J

"THOUSAND MILE WALK TO THE GULF"

"REVISITED"

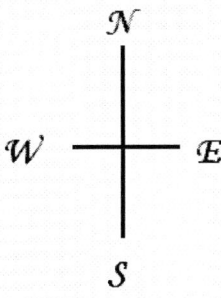

"Ramblin" Ron Boone

John Muir's Thousand Mile Walk to the Gulf "Revisited.
Copyright © 2006 by Ronald Boone. All rights reserved. No part of this publication may be reproduced, without written permission of the author. Correspondence regarding this work should be sent to Ronald Boone 25 Orchard Terrace Washington, PA 15301

All illustrations were by the author

ISBN 0910042969

The sketch on the front cover was drawn, by the author.

Printed in the United States of America.

CONTENTS

Illustrations   5

Preface   6

1. INDIANA   11
   Indianapolis   12
   Jeffersonville   13

2. KENTUCKY   16
   Louisville   16
   Elizabethtown   20
   Munfordville   23
   Glasgow Junction   25
   Glasgow   26
   Burkesville   28

3. TENNESEE   29
   Jamestown   31
   Montgomery   34
   Kingston   34
   Philadelphia   36
   Madisonville   38

4. NORTH CAROLINA   42
   Murphy   42

5.	GEORGIA	44
	Blairsville	44
	Gainesville	46
	Athens	47
	Thompson	49
	Augusta	50
	Savannah	56
6.	FLORIDA	61
	Fernandina	61
	Gainesville	67
	Cedar Key	70

Endnotes	77
Index	79

ILLUSTRATIONS

John Muir's Route Map, (Reproduction)	10
Jeffersonville Train Station	14
Louisville to Elizabethtown Map	18
My Old Kentucky Home	19
White Snakeroot	21
Brown-Pusey House	22
Bell's Tavern 'Ruins'	26
Public Resolution Document	27
Roan County Court House	35
Gideon Morgan House	36
Town Square, Philadelphia, Tennessee	37
Train Station, Thompson, Georgia	50
Bonaventure Cemetery	58
Florida House Inn	64
Sheet-Iron Salt Kettle	72

PREFACE

On September 22, 2003, a black and white '*Stonewall*' gelding named Domino, drawing a specially designed carriage, with a yellow canopy, clopped his way out of Anchorage, Kentucky, a residential suburb of Louisville. Domino was about to embark on a trip that would cover a thousand miles, ending in Cedar Key, Florida. On board the carriage, designed for the physically challenged, were Cindy Goff and the carriage designer, Michael Muir, who also developed the '*Stonewall*' horse breed. The purpose of their trip was to demonstrate how the use of horses lends to a unique therapy for people with disabilities. This physically challenged duo would follow the route walked by Michael's great-grandfather, the renowned naturalist John Muir, who in 1867 took a thousand mile walk from Louisville, Kentucky to Cedar Key, Florida, on the Gulf of Mexico where he gathered botanical samples along the way.

When I visited Yosemite Valley and the giant Redwoods and Sequoias of America's north-west, I gave humble thanks to John Muir and his noble efforts to successfully preserve their grandeur. I, like many others generally associated John Muir with California and the forests of the west coast.

I was taken aback when I visited the Florida State Museum at Cedar Key and saw a marker indicating that John Muir (1838-1914), made the thousand mile walk in 1867. He was twenty nine years old.

The account of John Muir's 1867 walk was chronicled in his book, *John Muir, A Thousand Mile Walk to the Gulf.* In 1916, two years after Muir's death it was published by Muir's literary executor, William Fredric Bade (1871-1936). Bade was a professor of the Pacific School of Religion in Berkley, California. He was also the Sierra Club editor, director and a Muir protégé. After Muir's death, Bade was appointed his literary executor by Muir's daughters; Wanda and Helen; some of their children elected to maintain the Muir family name.

To publish, *A Thousand Mile Walk to the Gulf,* Bade used Muir's original journal – which included many penciled revisions, a type written draft and accounts of Muir's stay at Bonaventure Cemetery in Savannah.

After Bade's death, Linnie Marsh Wolfe, a friend of the Muir family was appointed his successor. Among her works are; *John of the Mountains,* and *The unpublished Journals of John Muir.*

At the Cedar Key Museum, I purchased the book; *John Muir, A thousand Mile walk to the Gulf.* This journal type account of his trip begins with a map of his route. This map identified every major town and city he visited. One look at this linear trail and I was hooked, I knew that I had to revisit John Muir's thousand mile walk to the Gulf.

In this work I used Muir's posthumously published version of, *A Thousand Mile Walk to the Gulf.* Also consulted were historic maps and documents of the 1867 period as well as libraries and historical societies as I followed along Muir's route.

Muir's route was not followed on foot, but rather in my 'mini' camper that I call *"Sheltowee",* a name given to Daniel Boone by Shawnee Chief Black Fish, meaning *"Big Turtle"*.

Throughout his trip, Muir leaves the established roadways and sets off into wilderness thickets. In an effort to follow Muir, I consulted maps and map features, reviewed descriptions in his journal entries and, at times, engaged in dead reckoning to arrive at the next town depicted on his route map.

To my dismay there were several towns mentioned in Muir's journal that did not appear on any recent maps. I would later discover their fate. I also found interesting bits of information along his route that occurred, prior to and after 1867.

Along the way, Muir often identifies many plant species, generally using their scientific names. As I traveled, I wondered what plants that Muir encountered are now missing from the landscape and what new plants have been carelessly introduced, like the troublesome Kudzu.

One can only speculate of what the post civil war landscape was like after years of battle, where savaging murderous thugs still roamed the countryside.

As I followed along Muir's route I tried to mentally determine what features would have been present in 1867. Split-rail and stone fences laced the countryside; barbed wire was only patented in 1867. The citizenry were using horses and wagons and the railroads were being restored, especially in the south. There were no electric lights as Thomas Edison (1847-1931), would not introduce the incandescent light-bulb until 1879. In 1867, Alfred Nobel (1833-1896) would patent dynamite.

During my research for this trip I would mention Muir to some folks that I encountered along the way and I was met with blank stares. However, all of the folks at the libraries and historical societies were cordial and very helpful. The following people were even supportive of my efforts; Robert Bailey, Roan County Heritage Commission in Kingston, Tennessee. Debby Barron, East Central Georgia Regional Library in Augusta, Georgia. Mary Lou Tucker, Yulee, Florida. Charles Neese, Cedar Key State Museum, Cedar Key, Florida. And Peggy Rix, Cedar Key Museum Curator, Cedar Key, Florida. My meeting with Peggy included a tour of the museum, as they were preparing several new installations, including one about John Muir.

My research also found another book with a similar theme, *John Muir's Longest Walk,* by the late photographer John Earl. It is a collection of award winning quality photographs, interlaced with excerpts from Muir's *Thousand Mile Walk to the Gulf.* While at a campground in Florida, I met Monte Zucker, a photographer friend of John Earl, who spoke very kindly of Earl and his professionalism.

Unless otherwise noted, all of John Muir's quotes in this work are from, *A Thousand Mile Walk to the Gulf.*

This revisit of Muir's walk ends at Cedar Key Florida. Muir continued on to Cuba, but still feeling ill from his 'malaria fever' he turned to New York City then headed west to California.

As one follows along on this adventure, perhaps they can step back into a time where life was a struggle in a land recovering from the Civil War; a war that destroyed much of the landscape and left despair in the hearts and minds of those caught up in it. This strife, in the south would take decades to fade. While on his walk, Muir gathered and studied many botanical specimens which he would, periodically, send back home for future study. On a lighter side, perhaps this work might encourage some readers to make visits to the places along Muir's route that, with some imagination, still exist as Muir found them.

1

INDIANA

After reading *John Muir's- Thousand mile walk to the Gulf,* I began planning the route that I would follow. I also prepared for the trip by reading *John Muir, rediscovering America.* By Fredrick Turner, Perseus Publishing, 10 East 53rd Street, New York NY 10022. Turner has presented a very comprehensive chronology of Muir's life and is an account well worth reading.

As I am about to follow Muir's 1867 walk perhaps it is appropriate at this time to give the reader a brief history of Muir's life up to this period: John Muir was born in Dunbar Scotland on April 21, 1838, and came to America, with his family in 1849, the year of the California Gold Rush. They settled in Wisconsin. He attended the University of Wisconsin, although no records exist that would show that he ever graduated. Muir was an inventor of sorts and built several types of clocks that he entered at the State Agricultural Fair in Madison. He went into Canada to 'botanize' and wait out the Civil War, to return in 1866. While in Canada he made mechanical improvements at the broom factory of William Trout and Charles Jay that surpassed production expectations. With his mechanical background Muir elected to settle in Indianapolis, Indiana because it had great industrial potential. Indianapolis was considered the cross roads of America because of the westward movement of traffic along the railroads and the national road.

In Indianapolis, Muir found work at the carriage factory of Osgood and Smith, which was located on south Illinois street.

Muir suffered an injury to his right eye rendering him blind for a brief period. During his convalescence, he contemplated his life and decided to leave the manufacturing theatre and engage in his future ambition of botanizing. (In 1869, Muir would put his mechanical expertise back into practice when he was hired by James Mason Hutchings, to rebuild and operate a saw-mill in Yosemite Valley).

To begin his new life, Muir planned to venture among the southern states and then travel on to South America, the Amazon River and beyond. At times Muir has been compared to the German naturalist, Alexander, Freiherr von Humbolt (1769-1859), who visited Cuba, explored most of the Amazon River basin, as well as America and Mexico. (The first European to travel down the Amazon was Gonzalo Pizarro, in 1540).

In 1868 Muir traveled to California where he spent many years botanizing at Yosemite and the Sierra Nevada Mountains. His genuine deep seated love for nature and its beauty made him the respected naturalist that he was to become. On June 4, 1892 the Sierra Club was formed. Muir served as its president until his death on December 23, 1914.

INDIANAPOLIS, INDIANA:

Today Indianapolis, (from the Greek: Polis = city), is the largest city in Indiana and the state capitol. It began as a wilderness camp in 1820. In 1825, the state capitol was moved from Corydon, in the southern part of the state, to the more centrally located; Indianapolis.

The national road came through Indianapolis in 1834 and the railroads followed in 1847. The Central Canal was completed along the White River in 1836, but failed due to the unstable geology along its banks.

Post Civil War Indianapolis had no paved streets. It suffered from pollution and sanitary problems from manufacturing companies, fertilizer plants, glue and starch factories as well as paper mills. During the period between 1860 to1870, epidemic diseases, such as typhoid, dysentery, measles and fever were prevalent. It is little wonder that Muir wanted to leave the city and venture into natures realm.

On September 1, 1867, while Muir was still in Indianapolis, he wrote letters of good-by to his friends and drew up his last will and testament, thereby settling his affairs.

His travel possessions included a comb, brush, towel, soap and a change of underclothing. Muir also carried with him a copy of Burn's poems, Milton's, *Paradise Lost* and a *New Testament.* [1] He wore a gray suit and no-doubt, hob nail shoes; which were typical of the period; the nails protected the leather soles from wear.

Muir also took with him, thirty dollars. The currency of 1867 consisted of the following:

1st. Copper; cent, half cent, (3 cent piece, silver and copper)
2nd Silver; dollar, half dollar, quarter dollar, dime, half-dime
3rd Gold; $20 piece, eagle, half eagle, quarter eagle, three-dollar piece, dollar. [2]

The daily wage at the time was about seventy-five cents.

"John Muir, Earth-Planet, Universe", was written on the inside cover of Muir's journal.

On Sunday, September 1, 1867, Muir began his trip south by taking a train from Indianapolis to Jeffersonville Indiana. He was twenty-nine years old.

After conducting my research in Indianapolis I began to follow Muir's route by taking Interstate 65 south. I arrived at Jeffersonville via the Hamburg Pike.

JEFFERSONVILLE, INDIANA:

Jeffersonville Indiana and the surrounding area along the Ohio River was settled in 1786 when Fort Finney was constructed. Around 1801, the town was named after Thomas Jefferson, (1743-1826), and incorporated as a city in 1839. From June, 1802 to

1811, Jeffersonville served as the seat of Clark County and regained that status again in 1878.

Jeffersonville grew out of the steamboat industry; in 1834 James Howard launched his first steamboat the Hyperion, (a Titan of Greek mythology-the father of Helios), on the banks of the Ohio River at Jeffersonville. Today the *Belle of Louisville,* a sternwheeler and the *Star of Louisville,* a cruise ship offer entertainment and cruises on the Ohio.

Present day Jeffersonville is protected by floodwalls which have large heavy gates that prevent the Ohio River from entering the town during high water.

The Ohio River is a geologically young river which was formed during the Pleistocene Epoch which ended ten-thousand years ago. It was formed when Ice age glaciers diverted the north flowing rivers, of the United States, west into the Mississippi.

With no mention in his journal of the Devonian fossil beds below Great Falls of the Ohio, it becomes apparent that Muir took no notice of them.

Train Station: Jeffersonville, Indiana

In Jeffersonville there exists a train station that may be similar to the one where Muir disembarked.

Muir spent the night in Jeffersonville then crossed the Ohio River to Louisville Kentucky, but there is no mention of how he crossed the river. The first bridge to Louisville, a railroad bridge, was not built until 1870. Apparently, Muir either hitched a ride with a private boat owner or took a craft of the Louisville and Jeffersonville Ferry Company. "In 1802, William Henry Harrison, (1773-1841), then governor of the Indiana Territory granted Marsden G. Clark a license for a ferry service at Jeffersonville. The same is true for Joseph Bowman. In 1820, Joseph White was also given approval to keep a ferry in Jeffersonville. In 1837 the three ferry franchises vested and in 1865 became owned by eleven investors and was called the Louisville and Jeffersonville Ferry Company".[3] The ferry's reached Louisville at Bear Creek, upstream of the Great Falls of the Ohio River.

I crossed the Ohio River via the John F. Kennedy Memorial Bridge and headed for the Louisville Historic District.

2

KENTUCKY

LOUISVILLE, KENTUCKY:

"I steered through the big city [Louisville] by compass without speaking a word to anyone. Beyond the city I found a road running southward and after passing a scatterment of suburban cabins and cottages I reached the green woods and spread out my pocket map* to rough-hew a plan for my journey."
John Muir September 2, 1867.

*In Bade's introduction to *A Thousand Mile Walk to the Gulf*, he indicates that Muir's map has not been found and probably no longer exists.

Travelers in the late 1700's tended to avoid Louisville which was known as a disease infested swamp.

The Falls of the Ohio were first surveyed by Thomas Bullitt in 1773.

Louisville was named in honor of Louis XVI (1754-1793) of France. He was guillotined on January 21, 1793. Col. George Rodgers Clark, (1752-1818), Revolutionary war officer established the first settlement at Louisville in 1778. He is buried in Louisville's Cave Hill National Cemetery.

Louisville was located along the water route from Pittsburgh, Pennsylvania to New Orleans, Louisiana. The Great Falls on the Ohio River restricted water traffic until the Portland Canal began in 1825 and opened in 1830 when the *Uncas* was locked through. All trade passed through Louisville and the city prospered. By 1839, Louisville had gas street lights.

In 1808, the famous artist and naturalist John James Audubon (1785-1851), established a general store in nearby Henderson Kentucky from 1810 to 1819. Alexander Wilson (1766-1813), considered to be the greatest ornithologist prior to Audubon, met the latter in Louisville in 1810 while traveling from Lexington to Nashville. Wilson also met American naturalist William Bartram (1739-1823). The Bartrams, father and son will be discussed later in this work.

On Muir's walk he was in awe of the magnificent Kentucky oak trees.

"I have seen oaks of many species in many kinds of exposure and soil, but those of Kentucky excel in grandeur all I ever before beheld".
John Muir, September 2, 1867.

"Everything about this old Kentucky home bespoke plenty, unpolished and unmeasured. The house was built in true Southern style, airy, large and with a transverse central hall that looks like a railroad tunnel and heavy rough outside chimneys".
John Muir, September 3, 1867.

Initially one might assume that Muir had visited the Old Kentucky Home in Bardstown. When reviewing Muir's previous journal entries he states,

"My plan was simply to push on in a general southward direction by the wildest, leafiest, and least trodden way I could find promising the greatest extent of virgin forest".
John Muir, September 2, 1867.

Had Muir been heading for Bardstown, which is southeast of Louisville, he would be traveling the Bardstown Road which was a relatively well traveled road at the time; hardly the least trodden direction.

Muir crossed the Salt River which he describes, *"as nearly dry".* Although the Salt River crosses the Bardstown Road near Smithville, Muir writes that;

"Much of my way this forenoon was over naked limestone".

John Muir, September 3, 1867.

Muir then notes, *"I came to a region of rolling hills called Kentucky Knobs – hills of denudation, covered with trees on the top".* The knobs that he was describing were no doubt the series of knobs, west of Lebanon Junction, located within the present day Fort Knox Military Reservation. Of these knobs the most notable are; Bolton Knob, Orms Knob, (782 ft.), and Stark Knob.

Muir then discusses a, *"Rocky stream [Rolling Fork]".* When Muir crosses Rolling Fork, he would have already passed Bardstown and The Old Kentucky Home.

Muir's Route, Louisville to Elizabethtown: Kentucky

In Muir's description of the *"Old Kentucky Home"*, he says that it had, *"rough outside chimneys"*, he was probably describing a similar home near the town of Booth or Colesburg.

My Old Kentucky Home: Bardstown, Kentucky

With the exceptions of the chimneys and a review of his route one would assume that Muir had visited Federal Hill; Judge John Rowan's home in Bardstown. Federal Hill has smooth chimneys that are integral with the house. The Rowan home was immortalized in the song," *My Old Kentucky Home, Goodnight"*, which was written by the Rowan's cousin, Stephen Collins Foster (1826-1864). It was published in 1853. There are hints that Foster was influenced by Harriet Beecher Stowe's, *"Uncle Toms Cabin, (1851)"*, Stowe's book may, no doubt have been, the inspiration for this song, because no documentation exists indicating that Foster ever visited Federal Hill.

On July 4, 1923 the Commonwealth of Kentucky established Federal Hill as "The Old Kentucky Home", and in 1928 the Kentucky Legislature made, *"My Old Kentucky Home",* the State song. The state of Florida also adopted one of Stephen Foster's songs; this will be discussed in the Florida chapter.

I was surprised to find that William P. Boone (1813-1875), reported to be a direct descendant of Daniel Boone (1734-1820), married the Rowans granddaughter, Eliza Harney. Today a portrait of William Boone hangs in the dining room at the Old Kentucky Home.

I continued driving south out of Louisville, on Fourth Street and began following local roads adjacent to Interstate 65, crossing the Salt River then Rolling Fork, then into Elizabethtown.

ELIZABETHTOWN, KENTUCKY:

"Walked southeast from Elizabethtown till wearied and lay down in the bushes by guess".
John Muir, September 3, 1867.

Elizabethtown was settled in 1779, by three pioneers from Virginia and was named for the wife of Andrew Hynes.

Thomas Lincoln (1778-1851); father of Abraham Lincoln (1809-1865), lived in Elizabethtown from 1796 to 1816, where in 1805 he helped build what is known today as the Lincoln Heritage House.

After the Lincoln family moved to southern Indiana, Abraham's mother, Nancy Hanks Lincoln (1784-1818), was reportedly stricken with "Milk Sickness", after drinking the milk from cows which have grazed on the poisonous White Snakeroot plant. White Snakeroot, *Eupatorium perfoliatum,* is a member of the sunflower family *asteraceae*. It was identified earlier as, *Eupatorium urticaefolium*. All parts of the plant are toxic and cause what was known as "puking fever" or "sick stomach". Today this condition is known as White Snakeroot intoxication. The disease claimed thousands of lives in the 1800s which supposedly included Nancy Hanks Lincoln who died on October 5, 1818 at the age of thirty-four.

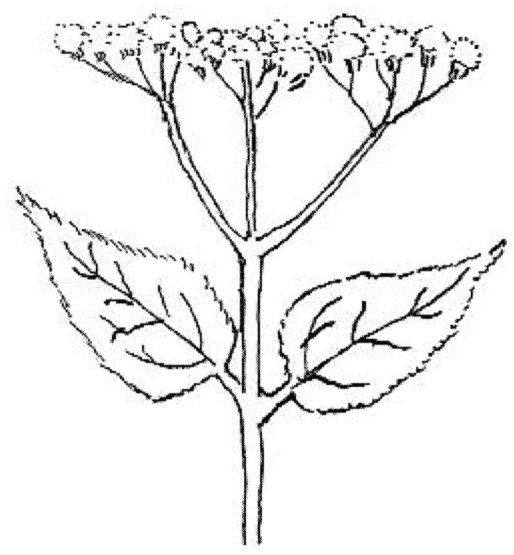

White Snakeroot, Eupatorium perfoliatum

The Lincoln family was quite well known in this Kentucky area and there is more information on Thomas Lincoln in the Burkesville section of this work.

Around the town square and adjoining side streets are structures of the 1867 period. One is represented by the Brown – Pusey House, which was built in 1825 and operated as a hotel called the Hill House. General George Armstrong Custer, (1839-1876), and his wife Elizabeth lived next door. Custer was assigned to Elizabethtown in 1871-73 to inspect and purchase horses for the army. In 1867-68, Custer was campaigning against the Cheyenne. On October 11, 1867 at Fort Leavenworth Kansas, a Court Marshal found Brevet Major General George Armstrong Custer, Lieutenant Colonel 7th Cavalry, guilty and sentenced him to suspension from rank and command for one year and forfeiture of his pay, for paying an unauthorized visit to his wife.

Brown-Pusey House: Elizabethtown Kentucky

    South of Elizabethtown, at the Hardin and Hart County line, Muir reached an imaginary point that was unknown in 1867; a Time Zone line. In 1867 there were more than fifty time zones in the United States. Up until the 1880's, every town established their own standard time, generally based on solar events. With the expansion of the railroads and trip scheduling, a better system of time keeping was required.

    A meteorologist named Cleveland Abbe needing a better method to share meteorological events with colleagues divided the United States into four time zones – similar to today. [The earths 360 degrees are divided onto 24 hours, which is equivalent to 15 minutes of arc for each hour]. This established the boundaries with variations necessary so as not to sub-divide major towns or cities. On November 18, 1883, the railroads, convinced by the Abbe process established standard time zones for their scheduling.

    Daylight Savings Time was initially used as a fuel saving measure during World War I. Standard Time and Daylight Savings

Time became law with the Standard Time Act of March 19, 1918. Daylight Savings Time was repealed in 1919, but was reestablished at the beginning of World War II and was observed throughout the war. In 1966, the Uniform Time Act standardized the time zones and dates for Savings Time.

Today, Standard Time is under the control of the United States Department of Transportation, because of its jurisdiction over transportation entities.

As I continued to follow John Muir I took US. Route 31-W south from Elizabethtown and made my way to Munfordville.

MUNFORDVILLE, KENTUCKY:

"Arrived about noon at Munfordville: was soon discovered and examined by Mr. Munford himself, a pioneer and father of the village".
John Muir, September 5, 1867.

Munfordville was founded in 1801 by Richard Jones Munford, when he arrived along the banks of the Green River at a place called Big Buffalo Crossing. In 1802, Munford began a ferry service across the river.

Today Munfordville, with a population of 1600, is the seat of Hart County.

The most notable feature of today's Munfordville are the various facades along main street that make it difficult to determine if buildings represent the 1867 era.

Traveling south on US. Route 31-W, I began to notice historic markers that told of Civil War battles. The highway and railroad run parallel as they head toward the town of Horse Cave. Horse Cave, with a present population of about 2,500, has a main street of older buildings, but I did not see any that would represent the 1867 period.

Continuing southwest I headed for Cave City and took Kentucky route 70 to the south entrance of Mammoth Cave National Park.

MAMMOTH CAVE:

"Arrived at the great Mammoth Cave. I was surprised to find it in so complete naturalness".
John Muir, September 6, 1867.

Mammoth Cave has been forming for thousands of years and will continue this process as long as the subterranean water continues to carry away the sub-surface geology.

When the underlying limestone, gypsum or dolomite dissolve beneath a land mass, depressions, sinkholes and caves are created to form something known as karst topography.

Mammoth Cave is a World Heritage site and has three-hundred-fifty miles of 'surveyed' passages. The cave laid idle for thousands of years, except for occasional visits by prehistoric people and was re-discovered in the late 1700s by European Americans. During the war of 1812, saltpeter; a component of gunpowder was mined here.

Mammoth Cave became a National Park in 1926, a year after it became an interest to the public with the death of Floyd Collins, a trapped cave explorer, who died before he could be rescued.

Today, the historic entrance to the cave, remains somewhat as Muir saw it in 1867.

I spent the night in the park, where I spoke with several folks. One lady, who lived nearby, confirmed my research that Glasgow Junction; which was Muir's next stop, is now known as Park City.

I arrived in Glasgow Junction in the morning.

GLASGOW JUNCTION, KENTUCKY:

"Started for Glasgow Junction. Got belated in the hill woods".
John Muir, September 6, 1867.

Glasgow Junction was located at the junction of a triple transportation hub; The Glasgow Road, The Bardstown Road and The Louisville-Nashville Pike. In 1827, it was initially known as Three Forks then re-named Glasgow Junction in 1863 when a railroad spur was completed from the Louisville-Nashville railroad to the town of Glasgow, eleven miles to the southeast.

In 1938, Glasgow Junction was re-named Park City when the railroads began to bring tourists to Mammoth Cave National Park.

A stage coach stop was established at Three Forks in 1827, and in 1830, William Bell built a tavern to accommodate the visitors to Mammoth Cave. Bells Tavern soon became internationally famous. The tavern burned in 1860 and was never restored. The ruins still exist and are identified with a historical marker.

While taking a tour of this great little village, a man at the lumber yard also confirmed the towns name switch.

Since I believed that Muir followed the railroad to Glasgow, I tried to follow as close as I could with a similar route. I took U.S.31-West toward Cave City then south on 2189. After crossing the present day CSX railroad I continued on to U.S.68 and followed it into Glasgow.

Bells Tavern Ruins: Glasgow Junction, Kentucky

GLASGOW, KENTUCKY:

"Glasgow is one of the few Southern towns that show ordinary American life'.
John Muir, September 7, 1867.

It was near Glasgow where Muir spent the night at the home of a well to do farmer.

Glasgow is the seat of Barren County and is about one third of its original size. It was established in 1799 and named by Scottish settlers from Virginia.

Driving out of Glasgow there are road signs designating the present day highway 90 as The John Muir Highway. At the Cumberland County court house in Burkesville, Kentucky there exists a resolution, (enacted on December 8, 1998), that renames the existing Highway 90W, once known as The Burkesville-Glasgow Road to The John Muir Highway.

> **ORDERS** — CUMBERLAND COUNTY FISCAL **COURT**
>
> REGULAR Term, Day, 8TH. Day of DECEMBER 19 98 CONT.
>
> Upon motion by Branham, Seconded by Long, it is hereby ordered and the Court hereby adopts the following Resolution, to-wit:
>
> ### RESOLUTION
>
> A resolution endorsing the historic name of John Muir Highway to be adopted by the State Transportation Cabinet to replace the existing Highway 90 W., now known as the Burkesville Glasgow Road.
>
> WHEREAS, John Muir, a naturalist of early times, who appreciated nature's beauty in our area, walked one thousand miles from Louisville, Kentucky, to the Gulf of Mexico in the late 1800's and,
>
> WHEREAS, John Muir wrote of his adventures and discoveries along his journey including inspiring words of the beauty of our local scenery; and,
>
> NOW, THEREFORE, BE IT RESOLVED, by the Fiscal Court of the County of Cumberland, Commonwealth of Kentucky, to endorse the historic name of John Muir Highway for Kentucky Highway 90 W, in Cumberland County, Kentucky.
>
> Enacted this 8 day of Dec, 19 98.
>
> Larry C. Hoots, County Judge Executive
>
> ATTEST:
> Betty L. Hogan, County Court Clerk
>
> Motion carried unanimously.

Public Resolution Document: Cumberland County, Kentucky

Continuing to follow Muir, I departed Glasgow on this highway. Along the way there was a welcome sign for the town of Burkesville which read, "The Best Kept Secret in Kentucky".

When I reached Burkesville I visited Smiths Pharmacy, which is reported to be the oldest in the state.

BURKESVILLE, KENTUCKY:

"Burkesville, in beautiful location, is embosomed in a glorious array of verdant flowing hills".
                John Muir, September 8, 1867.

Burkesville, the seat of Cumberland County who's Post Office opened in 1801 was incorporated in 1846, and named after Samuel Burke.

Thomas Lincoln, father of President Abraham Lincoln, was the constable of Cumberland County from 1802 to 1804. It is also reported that he owned land on the Cumberland River and on Marrowbone Creek.

Due to its location along the Columbia River, many Civil War battles were fought to gain control of this area. These battles resulted in a decline of the counties economy and remained so for quite some time.

In Bade's introduction to, *A Thousand Mile Walk to the Gulf",* he discusses a letter that Muir wrote in which he indicates that he covered about twenty-five miles a day.

"I walked from Louisville, a distance of one hundred and seventy miles, and my feet are sore".

Before Muir crossed the state line into Tennessee he made the following comment.

"Kentucky is the greenest, leafiest state I have yet seen".
                John Muir, September 9, 1867.

I continued east on Route 90 to the town of Snow, then took U.S. Route 127 south. As I traveled I saw tobacco drying in make-shift sheds.

3

TENNESSEE

When crossing into Tennessee one will find a lone cottage with two flag poles in the yard. One pole displays the American flag and the other; the stars and bars. You then realize that you have entered the Confederacy.

From July 4, 1867 to July 3, 1877, the flag of the United States had thirty-seven stars.

Because of its large Unionist population and its submission to Congressional demands, Tennessee was the only southern state to escape the harsh reconstruction measures of 1867 and was not placed under military rule.

At the Tennessee state line, U.S. Route 127 is named The Alvin York Highway. Alvin Cullum York, (1887-1964), was born in Pall Mall, Tennessee on December 13, 1887. He joined the Army in 1917, even though he was a conscientious objector. During World War I, he and seven other American soldiers captured 132 of the German enemy. His efforts were rewarded in a promotion to sergeant and he became a recipient of the Congressional Medal of Honor. York's Grist Mill is located along the highway at Pall Mall.

At this point in his trip, when comparing ferns, Muir writes.

"In Wood's and Gray's Botany, (Osmunda cinnamomea) is said to be a much larger fern than, (Osmunda Claytoniana). John Muir, September 10, 1867.

This entry also includes a footnote: "Alphonso Wood, *Class-book of Botany, with a Flora of the United States and*

Canada. The copy of this work carried by Muir on his wanderings is still extant. The edition is that of 1862".

Alphonso Wood, (1810-1881), graduated from Dartmoth in 1834. In 1867 he settled in West Farms, New York. He published, *Class Book of Botany,* in 1845 and *First Lesson in Botany,* in 1848.

An associate of Wood was fellow botanist Asa Gray who deserves mention at this point.

Asa Gray, (1810-1888), considered the Father of American Botany, initially studied Medicine, then botany. He published, *Elements of Botany,* in 1836; it was re-published as, *Botanical Textbook,* in 1853, it is now called, *Structural and Systematic Botany,* 1858. Gray also published, *Field, Forest and Garden Botany,* in 1867.

Gray has been credited with introducing Darwin's, *Theory of Natural Selection*, in the United States. Asa Gray and Charles Darwin (1809-1882), carried on a long-time correspondence. Gray, at the request of Darwin, often reviewed the latter's work and sent back comments. Gray received a copy of, *"The Origin of Species"*, at Christmas in 1859. Gray was a catalyst in getting it published in the United States. Much controversy erupted over Darwin's theory, especially from, according to Darwin's correspondence, the Swiss-American naturalist, Jean Louis Rodolphe Agassiz (1807-1873).

Asa Gray also theorized that North America and Asia were once geographically connected long before German Meteorologist Alfred Wegener (1880-1930), demonstrated that the continents could fit together into a giant land mass that he called, *Pangaea.* The theory was resurrected in the 1960s and now, through modern research, is now accepted as "Plate Tectonics". Other scientists also theorized the shifting of continents; most notably was an American, Frank B. Taylor (1860-1938).

In April 1872, Asa Gray, along with his wife, visited Muir in Yosemite. They spent a week together, botanizing. Gray invited Muir to teach at Harvard; Muir declined the offer.

With Muir's use of scientific identification, it is at this point; appropriate to mention Swedish Naturalist Carl von Linne (1707-1778), (generally known by his Latinized name; Carolus Linnaeus). Who developed, by using Latin and Greek; Linnaean Taxonomy – a system of scientific classification that he published in 1755 titled Systema Naturae. He also originated the symbols for male and female; the shield and arrow signifying, (Mars) and the hand mirror for, (Venus). He also helped develop the Celsius Temperature Scale.

Before I reached Jamestown, I saw large expanses of timbered land. Muir was angered when, on his Wisconsin farm, he saw trees cut down and left to rot, only to make way for farming.

JAMESTOWN, TENNESSEE:

"Passed the poor rickety, thrice-dead village of Jamestown, an incredibly dreary place".
John Muir, September 10, 1867.

In 1823, Fentress County was established and named to honor James Fentress. Then in 1828, Sand Springs was renamed, Jamestown once again to honor Fentress.

John M. Clemens resided in Jamestown in the 1830s, where he worked as, among other endeavors, County Commissioner. He was also the Post Master at Pall Mall from 1832 until 1835, when he moved to Missouri, where his son Samuel was born. Samuel Clemens, better known as, Mark Twain, (1835-1910) was lecturing in New York City when Muir took his walk in 1867.

The Governor of Tennessee in 1867 was William G. Brownlow.

Upon leaving present day Jamestown, one might find a stand of tall grasses with white flowery heads – Muir would have been elated.

After a meager meal of cornbread and bacon, Muir's host asked him what he was doing in the south. Muir replied that he was looking for plants.

"Oh, all kinds; grass, weeds, flowers, trees, mosses, ferns, - almost everything that grows is interesting to me".
John Muir September 10, 1867.

About fifteen miles south of Jamestown, near present day Brewstertown, Muir, again crossed the time zone boundary.

When Muir asks about the availability of accommodations toward North Carolina, he was told. "Yes, its only two miles to the next house, but beyond that there are no houses that I know of, except empty ones who's owners have been killed or driven away during the war". [From, *A Thousand Mile Walk to the Gulf,* on September 10, 1867].

"Houses are far apart and uninhabited, orchards and fences in ruins – sad marks of war".
John Muir, September 11, 1867.

Muir, no doubt passed the remnants of homesteads where war veterans, many amputees, returned to only blackened chimneys.

The United States Civil War basically began in the 1830s as a 'Cold War', and became increasingly heated until open conflict broke out on April 12, 1861, with the attack on Fort Sumter, South Carolina. The war ended when Robert Edward Lee, (1807-1870), surrendered at 3:45 PM on Psalm Sunday, April 9, 1865, in the home of Wilmer McLean at Appomattox.

The Civil War resulted in over 600,000 casualties of both the North and South.

The south was set back one generation because of the war. It lost nearly one half of its livestock; it would take twenty-five years before the number of livestock, in the south, would return to pre-war levels. Industry and the railroads were in shambles. The war would not be forgotten until 1940, when everyone that remembered it had died. Today, for some reason, there are some that will never let this war end.

The Congressional Reconstruction Act of 1867 divided the eleven Confederate States into five military districts, with the exception of Tennessee as mentioned earlier.

It was not until 1910 that the total cost of the war was realized by the federal government to be 11.5 billion dollars, which included veteran benefits and pensions.

Muir entered the south during Congressional Reconstruction, which lasted from 1867 until it lost momentum after about twenty years.

During Muir's trip, the south was being invaded by northerners attempting to gain wealth from the spoils of the war; these were the carpetbaggers – southern republicans, doing the same, were called scallywags.

The following will reflect the realities in the south at the time of Muir's walk.

"And so in 1867, Uncle Jesse returned and found her and the children free, and thriving, in the same cabin in which he left them, though the big house was vacant, and the plantation in new hands".

"At that time, Southern States were rife with utter lawlessness and bitter animosities; and acts of malicious and cruel outrage were frequent occurrences. Thus the worst elements and characteristics of every class were made prominent".[4]

Muir was confronted by ten men on horseback. He smiled, looked them in the face, said, "Howdy", walked around them and kept walking. The following is his account.

"They all were mounted on rather scrawny horses, and all wore long hair hanging down on their shoulders. Evidently they belonged to the most irreclaimable of the guerrilla bands who, long accustomed to plunder, deplored the coming of peace. I was not followed, however, probably because the plants projecting from my plant press made them believe that I was a poor herb doctor, a common occupation in these mountain regions".
John Muir, September 11, 1867.

I took route 52 out of Jamestown to the town of Elgin where I took U.S. 27 south, toward Montgomery, Tennessee; a town that I could not find.

MONTGOMERY, TENNESSEE:

"Passed Montgomery, a shabby village at the head of the east slope of the Cumberland Mountains".
John Muir, September 12, 1867.

The town of Montgomery no longer exists. In fact there were two towns by the name Montgomery which were both the county seat of Morgan County. The county was created in 1817 and the county seat was named in honor of Major Montgomery, who was killed in 1814 while serving with Andrew Jackson, (1767-1845). The first town was located along the Knoxville-Nashville Turnpike. A pile of rocks, from the courthouse chimney are all that remain of the first Montgomery. In 1826, the second Montgomery had become the Morgan County seat; this is the town that Muir passed through.

After 1845, nearby Wartburg gradually grew to become the dominant town in the area. In 1870, Wartburg became the County Seat and Montgomery became a ghost town.[5]

During Muir's visit, the sheriff at Montgomery was J.H. Byrd, who served from 1866 to 1868. The Clerk of County Courts was John L. Scott; 1864 to1874.

I left the Montgomery area and continued south on U.S. 27 to Interstate 40 then east to Kingston.

KINGSTON, TENNESSEE:

"Reached Kingston before dark. Sent back my plant collection by express to my brother in Wisconsin".
John Muir, September 12, 1867.

Kingston Tennessee has the unique distinction of being the state capitol for one day; September 21, 1807.

The historic antebellum court house was built in 1854 and still stands today where it serves as the Roan County Museum of History.; (antebellum from Latin = "before the war", generally considered as the period from 1812 to 1860).

I met Robert Bailey of the Roan County Heritage Commission, which is located in the historic court house. He was quite helpful in confirming the Montgomery history. He also pointed out a few historic structures from the 1867 period; such as the Gideon Morgan House, circa 1812, which is located across the street from the court house. It is reported to be the oldest house in Roan County. Perhaps Muir passed between the two buildings on his trip south.

Roan County Court House: Kingston, Tennessee

Gideon Morgan House: Kingston, Tennessee

In 1777, the Duke of Orleans – later Louis Philippe of France, passed through Kingston while on his way to Nashville. His trip was organized by President George Washington.

I departed Kingston on route 58 and traveled south-west to route 72, taking it to Louden. I then took U.S. 11 south to Philadelphia, which is located on the Roane and Monroe County line.

PHILADELPHIA, TENNESSEE:

"Philadelphia is a very filthy village in a beautiful situation".
  John Muir, September 14, 1867.

In the fall of 1821, William Knox and Jacob Pearson laid off seventy town lots and named the town, New Philadelphia.[6]

In 1828, it was established as a town by the General Assembly of Tennessee.

Today the town square, home of the Post Office and Library, appears to be deserted and in disarray, only because of the abandoned store across from the railroad. The library was small and had no desk; only a chair for this writer to use while gathering data.

Town Square: Philadelphia, Tennessee

Along the road out of Philadelphia there are several stone homes that well represent the 1867 period.

From Philadelphia I followed U.S. 11, south to the town of Sweetwater, Tennessee, turned left onto Old State Road 68 to College road then south into Madisonville.

MADISONVILLE, TENNESSEE:

"Walked through many a leafy valley, shady grove and cool brooklet. Reached Madisonville, a brisk village".
John Muir, September 14, 1867.

In 1819 the town of Madisonville was known as Tellico it became Madisonville in 1830.

The first news paper in Madisonville was the *Tennessean,* published by Henderson, Johnson and Jordan in 1833.

Madisonville was the birthplace of Estes Kefauver (1903-1963), who in 1949 became a senator from Tennessee.

The mention of Tellico brings to mind, the Tellico Dam construction and the controversy over the endangered Snail Darter.

North east of Madisonville lies the 16,500 acre – thirty mile long, Tellico Lake which was formed when The Tennessee Valley Authority planned to build a hydroelectric power dam on the Little Tennessee River. Construction began in 1967 and in 1973 the project was placed in the national spotlight after an ichthyologist (one who studies fish), discovered a three-inch long Perch called the Snail Darter. It was found that the entire species lived in the Little Tennessee River and would be impacted by the proposed dam. The Snail Darter was then listed as an endangered species and the construction of the Tellico Dam came to a halt. Plaintiffs argued that the Tennessee Valley Authority was violating The Endangered Species Act and the federal courts agreed. The project was 80% completed at the time. At this point Congress spent more than $100 million on the dam and continued to provide funding for mitigation of the Snail Darter and its habitat, even though provisions in the Endangered Species Act, allowed no exceptions. The Endangered Species Act of 1973 (16 U.S.C. 1531-1543), was to conserve the ecosystems upon which endangered and threatened species depend.

In mid- 1979, using a shrewd tactic to circumvent the law, Senator Howard Baker and Congressman John Duncan, both from Tennessee, buried a small provision into a large piece of legislation that would allow the Tellico project to be completed, which it was in late-1979.

No Snail Darter survived in that part of the Little Tennessee River impounded by the dam. There were however, small populations surviving elsewhere on the river. The Department of the Interior, in light of this situation moved the Snail Darter from the endangered list to the threatened list.[7]

Later in life, Muir would also lead the cause to halt the construction of a dam across the Hetch Hetchy Valley near Yosemite in California, an area that he first explored in 1871.

On December 6, 1913, the U.S. Senate granted the city of San Francisco the use of Hetch Hetchy Valley as a water supply reservoir. On December 19, 1913, President Woodrow Thomas Wilson signed it into law. Probably due to this emotional, personal loss, John Muir died a year later on December 24, 1914.

It was near Madisonville where Muir crossed the trail of an earlier explorer; Hernando De Soto (1500?-1542). During his exploits of the southern United States, De Soto made his way through the Tennessee area around 1540-41. He was followed by another Spanish expedition of Juan Pardo, (?), in 1566-68, who mined for gold in the Hiawassee and Tennessee River valleys.

De Soto was offered fresh water pearls from the indigenous people to the east. In his quest for gold he treated the native population horribly; stealing food, burning villages and taking many captive. Killing thousands outright, De Soto also killed thousands more in a sinister yet unknowingly way by infecting them with European diseases for which they had no immunity.

De Soto passed abandoned villages, whose inhabitants died off several years earlier from epidemics that were spread by infected peoples from along the Atlantic coast.

"Prior to 1492, America had an estimated twenty million inhabitants; since Columbus, ninety-five percent perished from disease".[8]

De Soto, himself died of a fever and was secretly buried along the banks of the Mississippi River so that he would appear to be immortal. (Some reports claim that he was buried in the Mississippi River).

Beyond Madisonville, Muir discusses the area.

"This is the most primitive country I have seen, primitive in everything.
John Muir, September 17, 1867.

An old gentleman says to Muir, "You, who are traveling for curiosity and wonder, ought to see our gold mines". Muir writes,

"I agreed to stay and went to the mines. Gold is found in small quantities throughout the Alleghenies".
John Muir, September 16, 1867.

Gold was the reason that the government relocated the Cherokee from this area to Oklahoma. It was near here that Muir crosses the, "Trail of Tears", of 1838. The Trail of Tears will be discussed in greater detail in the North Carolina chapter.
With the following statement Muir tells of the financial dealings of the local peoples.

"But coffee was the greatest luxury which these people knew. The only way of obtaining it was by selling skins or, in particular, 'sang', that is ginseng, which found a market in far-off China".
John Muir, September 19, 1867.

This entry in, *A Thousand Mile Walk to the Gulf,* includes Bade's following footnote: "Muir's journal contains the following additional note: M. County produces $5000 worth a year of ginseng root, valued at seventy cents a pound. Under the law, it is not allowed to be gathered until the first of September".
Ginseng native to China is a stimulant and supposed aphrodisiac. The American variety, *Panax, quinquefolius,* is sometimes substituted for the Chinese variety. It was the earliest marketable herb to be harvested in the United States. Some roots can be a century old. Recently, ginseng is selling for, between $250 to $500 per pound in China and Japan.

"In 1770, it was estimated that the colonies exported 74,605 pounds of the roots, mostly to Asia. Even Daniel Boone collected and sold ginseng".[9]

"Boone was no sooner home, however than with his boys as pole men and Rebecca as cook, he piloted a keelboat back upstream loaded with fifteen tons of ginseng root. 'Sang', as everyone on the frontier called it, fetched a good price from American apothecaries and shippers who sent it to China".[10]

In a boating mishap, the 'sang' was nearly ruined and Boone received less than one half of his expected price.

I took route 68 south from Madisonville.

In southwestern Tennessee I began to see mountains as I crossed the Tellico Plains and entered the Cherokee National Forest, where in 1827, gold mining was taking place.

In Polk County, the area featured mixed pine and hardwood trees on both sides of the very winding road.

I can not say that I was lost on this portion of the trip, but I was bewildered for about an hour; which did not matter much because the scenery was great.

I continued to follow route 68 south through the town of Tellico Plains, then crossing the Hiwassee River and on to the town of Farmer. South of Farmer I took route 123 to the North Carolina state line, where Tennessee route 123, becomes North Carolina route 294. I continued along route 294, passing through the Nathanalia National Forest. When I reached U.S. 64, I turned east and traveled into Murphy, North Carolina.

4

NORTH CAROLINA

North Carolina gained statehood on November 21, 1789. It seceded from the Union during the Civil War and was re-admitted on July 4, 1868. The governor at the time of Muir's trip was Jonathan Worth, who served from 1865 to 1868.

MURPHY, NORTH CAROLINA

"In Murphy I was hailed by the sheriff who could not determine by my colors and rigging to what country or craft I belonged".
John Muir, September 19, 1867.

Murphy is situated along the Hiwassee River with, present day, Lake Hiwassee nearby. Murphy was first called Huntersville, then Huntington around 1821.

In 1828, a trading post was built along the river. It was finally named Murphy after Archibald D. Murphey; due to a paper error at one point, the "e" was omitted.

Murphy is located in Cherokee County, with the Cherokee Indian Reservation sixty miles to the north-east. In 1838, after gold was discovered in Dahlonega, Georgia, more than 15,000 Cherokee Indians were removed by the U.S. Army from North Carolina, Georgia, Tennessee and Alabama. They were forced to leave their ancestral homelands and make a thousand mile trek to Oklahoma. This forced march began in Murphy at Fort Butler, which was built in 1837-38, by General Winfield Scott (1786-1866). The fort was named for B.F. Butler, Secretary of War. For a time it served as the Court House. Muir visited Fort Butler while in Murphy.

> *"All day among the groves and gorges of Murphy with Mr. Beal. Was shown the site of Camp Butler where General Scott had his headquarters when he removed the Cherokee Indians to a new home in the West".*
> *John Muir, September 20, 1867.*

The Cherokee removal march would follow the Unicoi Turnpike which was a wagon road that opened in 1816. It is likely that Muir traveled, at least a portion of the Unicoi.

Thousands of Cherokee died during this removal to Oklahoma. They called it, "nunahi-Duna-Dlo-Hilu-I"; which translates into, "Trail Where They Cried". It is known today as "The Trail of Tears".

While in Murphy I visited several historic sites, one being the Harshaw Chapel, circa 1860, and its adjoining cemetery.

After seeing Holly for the first time and having a lesson on 'dipping', snuff, Muir crossed the state line into Georgia and on into Blairsville.

I departed Murphy on U.S. 129 south and soon crossed the North Carolina-Georgia State line. Traveling south for another nine miles, I reached Blairsville, Georgia.

5

GEORGIA

In 1733, England established the first permanent settlement in Georgia at Savannah.

On January 19, 1861, Georgia seceded from the Union and on July 15, 1870 was readmitted.

In 1867, Joel Chandler Harris, (1848-1908), began writing stories, using authentic dialect, in the *Atlanta Constitution,* of the exploits of, 'Brer Rabbit, Brer Fox' and other characters, known as *The Tales of Uncle Remus.*

The Reconstruction Act of 1867 divided the eleven Confederate states into military districts and when Muir entered Georgia he entered the Military District of Union General John Pope (1822-1892), which included both Georgia and Florida.

BLAIRSVILLE, GEORGIA:

"Blairsville, which I passed in the forenoon seems a shapeless and insignificant village, but grandly encircled with banded hills".
John Muir, September 21, 1867.

Blairsville, the seat of Union County is located entirely within the Chattahoochee National Forest and was named for Captain James Blair (1761-1839).

Blairsville was created on December 3, 1832 and incorporated in 1847; the early settlers were farmers and gold miners.

Beyond Blairsville Muir writes;

"I reached the last mountain summit on my way to the sea. It is called the Blue Ridge."
John Muir, September 22, 1867.

Muir had also reached the location of the, present day Appalachian Trail. It began in 1921 and opened as a continuous hiking trail in 1937, extending from Springer Mountain, Georgia to Mt. Katahdin, Maine, a distance of 2,174 miles; due to on-going trail improvements and realignments this distance changes. The trail is under the supervision of the National Park Service and is, in part, maintained by various hiking clubs.

"Reached Mount Yonah in the evening".
John Muir, September 22, 1867.

Mount Yonah is located in the Chattahoochee National Forest, which was dedicated on July 9, 1936, but is surrounded by private land. The name of the mountain is from the Cherokee, Yanu, meaning bear, because of its shape.

The mountain is situated between the towns of Cleveland, and Helen, Georgia. In 1857, Cleveland was named Yonah. Present day Helen; named for a railroad surveyors daughter, has taken the form of a Bavarian village, which is hoped to attract tourists.

Col. Benjamin Hawkins (1754-1816), a United States Senator and Creek Indian Agent, visited this area in 1796.

Following U.S. 129 south from Blairsville, I continued through the Chattahoochee National Forest. The road wound through hardwoods, pines and grapevines where for some distance I followed trucks hauling logs to the mills.

GAINESVILLE, GEORGIA:

"Passed the comfortable, finely shaded little town of Gainesville".
    John Muir, September 23, 1867.

  Gainesville was one of the few small towns that Muir complemented.
  Muir goes on to say; *"The Chattahoochee River is richly embanked with massive, bossy dark green Water Oaks".* Throughout his journal Muir addresses a variety of plants, but none get greater review than the Oak trees. It is little wonder that Muir had great interest in the giant Redwoods and Sequoias of the Pacific coast and we must be ever grateful for his efforts to protect these giants.
  "Gainesville was located and made the established seat, [of Hall County] on July 3, 1821. Previous to this time the settlement was known as 'Mule Camp Springs'". [11]
  With the discovery of gold, Gainesville became the trading center for the mines.
  Green Street was the main route through Gainesville. It had many trees and was a direct route to the mines and the town spring. Homes were later built along Green Street after 1880; no doubt it was part of Muir's route.
  "During 1865 and 1866 sporadic acts of violence were reported in the north Georgia area. Signs of returning to normal began to appear in 1866 and 1867.[12]
  A slashing, tearing triple tornado, third on record, cut Gainesville to the quick shortly after eight-O-clock on the almost mid-night-like morning of April 6, 1936. Nearly everything in an area four blocks in width, in the heart of Gainesville exploded in ruins. Red Cross close-out figures show 139 homes were destroyed, 198 damaged.[13]

  "Mr. Pratter accompanied me a short distance from the house and warned me over and over again to be on the lookout for rattlesnakes".
    John Muir, September 25, 1867.

Later that day Muir wrote, *"Rattlesnakes abundant".* This was the Timber Rattlesnake *Crotalus borridus*, which could be from 35 to 74 ½ inches long. These Southern varieties are yellowish, pinkish or brownish gray, with a black tail.

Continuing along U.S. 129 I left Gainesville and headed south-east toward Athens.

ATHENS, GEORGIA:

"Reached Athens in the afternoon, a remarkably beautiful and aristocratic town, containing many classic and magnificent mansions of wealthy planters". "This is the most beautiful town I have seen on the journey, so far, and the only one in the South that I would like to revisit".
John Muir, September 26, 1867.

Athens, the largest city in north-east Georgia was incorporated in 1806. It became the seat of Clarke County in 1870.

The city of Athens lost three-hundred men in the Civil War.

"By 1867, the former slaves were adjusting to their freedom and were purchasing homes, securing jobs, organizing a volunteer fire company and establishing churches".[14]

"Long zigzag walk amid the old plantations, a few of which are still cultivated in the old way by the same Negroes that worked them before the war, and who still occupy their former "quarters". They are now paid seven to ten dollars a month".
John Muir, September 27, 1867.

In Georgia after the Civil War, a common name for African American communities was, "Shermantowns"; after Civil War, Union commander, William Tecumseh Sherman (1820-1891).

The University of Georgia was incorporated on January 27, 1785. The campus was established in September of 1801.

"The history of the city, [Athens], and the university are so interrelated that it is impossible to consider them separately".[15]

One of the homes that Muir may have passed during his walk was the Church-Waddel-Brumby House; built in 1820, it is believed to be the oldest in Athens. It was moved to its present location and now serves as the Welcome Center.

One might encounter the Kudzu plant in Kentucky and as you travel south it becomes more abundant, with the Kudzu, "Mother Lode" being found in Athens where they proudly advertise, "The Kudzu Festival".

Kudzu is a plant that Muir did not encounter on his walk, for it was not introduced to the United States until 1876, by the Japanese during the Centennial Exposition in Philadelphia, Pennsylvania.

"Kudzu, *Pueraria, with, montania, thunbergiana or lobata,* grows at a rate of a foot a day and under ideal conditions, can grow sixty feet in a year. Herbicides have little effect on the plant, but, in some areas it is controlled by goats.

In the 1920s it was grown in Florida for animal forage. The soil Conservation service promoted the use of Kudzu for erosion control in the 1930s and in the 1940s farmers were paid to plant Kudzu.

The United States government discontinued the use of Kudzu in 1953 and declared it a weed in 1972.

A pest for the South-east, Kudzu has been used in the Orient for centuries as food and medicine".[16]

One plant that is more invasive than Kudzu is Cogon Grass, *Imperata cylinrica.*

One wonders, how long it will take the small Bamboo plants being sold today at American shopping malls to become invasive pests, or worse.

As Muir Traveled toward Thompson, Georgia he no doubt passed through, or at least near the town of Washington; it was not on his map. It is important to note here that Confederate President, Jefferson Davis (1808-1889), stopped in Washington while fleeing southward after the Civil War. On May 10, 1865, he was captured at a campsite near Irwinsville, Georgia; the rumor that Davis was captured while wearing women's clothing was not true and was created to humiliate the former president. Davis, along with his wife and children were taken to Macon, Georgia. They were then taken, by train, through Atlanta to Augusta, where they were put on a steamer and shipped down the Savannah River. Jefferson Davis was subsequently taken to Fort, [Fortress], Monroe, Virginia, on the Chesapeake Bay. [In 1865, Harriet Ross Tubman (1820-1913), one of the more famous, 'conductors', on the Underground Railroad; worked at Fortress Monroe as a nurse to wounded soldiers]. On May 13, 1867, Davis was released from custody, after a, reported $100,000, bond was posted by prominent Northern as well as Southern citizens; namely, Horace Greeley (1811-1872) and Cornelius Vanderbilt (1794-1877). After Jefferson Davis was released from Fortress Monroe, he traveled abroad then returned to live in Memphis Tennessee. In 1877, he settled in Biloxi, Mississippi where he would write, *The Rise and Fall of the Confederate Government,* 1881.

I departed Athens on U.S. 78, which was at one time called the Wrightborough Road which went from Athens to Washington and on to Augusta.

THOMPSON, GEORGIA:

"Between Thompson and Augusta I found many new and beautiful grasses, tall gerardias, liatris, club mosses, etc".
John Muir, September 30, 1867.

"The first mention of Thompson we find is in Adiel Sherwood's *Georgia Gazette,* of 1837 where he says, "Thompson is the name of a village or place of deposit, lately begun on the Georgia Railroad". Thompson was known as, "The Slashes".[17]

"Thompson was a small settlement called, Hickory Level; from the abundance of Hickory trees, and sometimes called, Frog Pond; because it was quite swampy. The whole town was once the property of John Langston, who had a large Plantation. The town was named Thompson in 1853. The first train depot was a wooden building, replaced by the present granite station in 1860; a later addition was constructed of brick".[18]

Train Station: Thompson, Georgia

Between Thompson and Augusta, is the small town of Harlem, Georgia; the birth place of Oliver Norvell Hardy Jr. (1892-1957). Hardy was an actor in Hal Roach comedies until 1927, when he teamed up with Stan Laurel-Arthur Stanley Jefferson, (1890-1965). As Laurel and Hardy they became the most successful comedy team making over one hundred movies.

AUGUSTA, GEORGIA:

"Traveled today more than forty miles without dinner or supper. No family would receive me, so I had to push on to Augusta".
                        John Muir, September 30, 1867.

Founded in 1736, four years after Savannah, Augusta is Georgia's second oldest city. It was an Indian trading post and the center for the tobacco trade. It served as the capitol of Georgia from 1785 until 1795.

William Tecumseh Sherman, by-passed Augusta when on his way to Savannah, therefore many of the older structures were not destroyed.

"In the spring of 1867, Foster Blodgett was appointed mayor".[19]

"After the walking wounded parade, came men on litters. Their bodies, their heads, their limbs wrapped in bloody, dirty bandages. Some of the blood was old and caked; some new and oozing. The dirt came from the battlefield, the field hospital, and from the smoke-belching locomotive on the long train ride. The litters were carried slowly by other dirty, grimy men. Tommy and his friends watched the procession and heard the soft, muffled moans of pain and human agony. The men on the litters looked alike, yet different. Their faces were pale beneath the dirt. Their eyes vacant, staring without seeing".[20]

Tommy witnessed this scene during the middle of the Civil War. A few years later, at the age of eleven, he may have observed a slender, worn and tattered John Muir entering Augusta.

Tommy was born in Staunton Virginia and relocated, as an infant, to Augusta with his Presbyterian minister father. He suffered from developmental dyslexia but overcame it as an adult. He began his formal education in 1866-1867, at Professor Joseph Tyrone Derry's Boys School. In 1867, Tommy's brother Jessie was born.

In 1913, Tommy became the 28th president of the United States; Tommy was Thomas Woodrow Wilson (1856-1924). Wilson lived in Augusta for thirteen years, leaving in 1871. His boyhood home is located at 419 Seventh Street in Augusta.

As mentioned in the Madisonville Tennessee section, it was Woodrow Wilson who in 1913 dealt the final blow to Muir's attempt to protect Hetch Hetchy Valley near Yosemite.

The Augusta Canal was built in 1845 and provided power for manufacturing, making Augusta one of the South's major industrial centers.

There were two newspapers in Augusta at the time of Muir's walk; *The Loyal Georgian,* - a black newspaper, and *The Weekly Loyal Georgian,* (August 10, 1867 to February 1868).

In his book *The Story of Augusta,* Edwin Cashin describes the Savannah River with the following; "Below Augusta the [Savannah] river twists and turns through low, marshy banks. There are few habitable sites along the river and not many places a road might cross. In fact, the Savannah is a long barrier which reaches from the mountains to the sea, blocking the way for any traveler, man or beast. The Rocks at the site of Augusta formed a crossing for buffalo, deer and other animals".[21]

"Found a cheap breakfast in a marketplace; then set off along the Savannah River to Savannah".
John Muir, October 1, 1867.

Upon leaving Augusta, Muir Followed the Savannah River, downstream; in doing so he would follow in the path of much earlier botanists; The Bartrams.

John Bartram (1699-1777), was a farmer, who had an interest in herbal botany. He would later be called the father of American botany. (As mentioned earlier; if Asa Gray was considered the father of American botany, then John Bartram should be considered the Grandfather of American Botany).

In 1728, Bartram started the first botanical garden in the United States at his new home at Kingessing on the Schuylkill River near Philadelphia, Pennsylvania. One day he watched in vain as the wind began to scatter the seeds of his European plants to the surrounding country-side. (In 1801, Dr. David Hosack (1769-1835), founded The Elgin Botanic Garden which was the first 'public' garden in the United States. This twenty acre garden was located at the site of the present day Rockefeller Center).

In 1733, Bartram formed a botanical trade enterprise with Peter Collinson, a London Quaker, merchant, amateur botanist and member of the Royal Society. Soon Bartram was providing American plant specimens to the aristocracy of England.

In 1743, John Bartram founded the American Philosophical Society with his friend Benjamin Franklin (1706-1790).

In 1765, Collinson persuaded King George III (1738-1820) of England to appoint John Bartram, botanist for the American Colonies; the position included a fifty pound annual salary. This monetary resource gave Bartram the opportunity to explore North and South Carolina, Georgia and Florida - John Bartram had already explored North America from Nova Scotia to Florida and from Lake Ontario to the Atlantic Ocean.

Bartram was later joined by his son William (1738-1823), who in his teen years was making sketches of flora and fauna.

In 1765, the Bertram's, using Savannah as a basic starting point, traveled the Savannah River to Augusta and beyond.

Visiting Augusta from 1765 to 1766, John Bartram and his son William, collected plants and observed the behavior of the indigenous people.

William Bartram describes Augusta with the following. "The village of Augusta is situated on a rich and fertile plain, in the Savannah River; the buildings are near its banks and extend nearly two miles up to the cataracts, or falls, which are formed by the first chain of rocky hills, through which this famous river forces itself".[22]

He also recorded the Black Oaks near Augusta as having a diameter of eleven feet and that they were straight for fifty feet up to their limbs.

From 1766 to 1776 he explored much of the area around Augusta, the Savannah River and much of north Florida.

William Bartram became famous with his book, *Travels,* (1791), highlighting his travels with his father. It was published by James and Johnson in Philadelphia with the Original title, *"Travels through North and South Carolina, Georgia, East and West Florida, the Cherokee country, the Extensive Territories of the Muscogules, or Creek Confederacy and the Country of the Choctaws"*. It was published in Britain in 1792 and in Germany and Ireland in 1793. The French publication came in 1799.

William Bartram, was invited by Thomas Jefferson (1743-1826), the third president of the United States, to join the Meriwether Lewis (1774-1809), and William Clark (1770-1838), expedition. Due to his age (65) and failing health, (an eye disease, reportedly from Scarlet Fever or a Poison Ivy infection) Bartram declined.

Muir would follow the Bartram's trail along the Savannah River and cross it again in Florida.

Also following the Bartram's route along the Savannah River was the French botanist, Andre Michaux (1746-1802 or 1803 in Madagascar, of a tropical fever). He was sent to America by Louis XVI of France, to find plants that could be cultivated in France. (In September of 1786, through Benjamin Franklin, he visited William Bartram at his garden at Kingessing).

Using Charleston, South Carolina as a base of operations, Michaux explored the South-Eastern United States, and in April through July of 1787 he traveled up the Savannah River to it's headwaters near North Carolina. In 1801, Michaux published, *The Oaks of North America,* this book would surely be of great interest to Muir.

Michaux was joined by a Scottish botanist, John Fraser (1750-1811). In 1797-98, Fraser was a botanical collector for the Czar of Russia. He also named several plants; the Fraser Magnolia, *Magnolia fraseri,* which grew in Georgia and the Fraser Fir, *Abies fraseri,* which is the official tree of North Carolina and was used as the Christmas tree of the White House, nine times.

Muir mentions the Magnolia while along the Savannah River, but not Fraser's.

"Almost all trees and shrubs are evergreens here with thick polished leaves. "Magnolia grandiflora", becoming common".
John Muir, October 8, 1867.

About twelve miles South of Augusta; near the Department of Energy, Savannah River Plant, near Shell Bluff, Georgia, Muir would again cross the route taken by Hernando DeSoto.

It was at Shell Bluff, Georgia, where John Bartram was to describe a giant fossil Oyster found in a deposit from the Eocene Epoch (37.5 million to 54 million years ago). It was later classified as *Ostrea georgiana.*

Muir made the following, journal entries describing the Savannah River:

October 2, "in a low bottom forest of the Savannah River".

October 3, "In Pine Barrens, most of the day".

October 4, "All day in dense, wet, dark, mysterious forest of flat-topped taxodiums".

October 5, "Saw the stately banana for the first time, growing luxuriantly in the wayside gardens".

October 6, "Immense Swamps still more completely fenced and darkened that never ruffled with winds or scorched with drought".

October 7, "Impenetrable taxodium swamp, seemingly boundless".

October 8, "Found the first woody compositae, a most notable discovery".

While Muir followed along the Savannah River, I traveled south from Augusta on U.S. 25 to Millen Georgia. Then I followed route 21 south to Savannah;

The Savannah River valley is quite flat with numerous Ox-bow lakes. Even today, there are very few river crossings between Augusta and Savannah. The ones that do exist are: Sand Bar Ferry Bridge near Augusta, U.S.301 at Burtons Ferry Landing, State route 119 near Tuckasee King Landing, Interstate 95, and U.S. 17, both near Savannah and U.S. 17 (Business) in Savannah. This lack of roads near the Savannah River is typical also in South Carolina.

SAVANNAH, GEORGIA:

"Reached Savannah, but found no word from home, and the money that I ordered to be sent by express from Portage [Wisconsin] by my brother had not yet arrived. Feel dreadfully lonesome and poor".
John Muir, October 8, 1867.

Muir spent the next six days wandering about Savannah waiting for his money to arrive.

Savannah was founded by James Edward Oglethorpe (1696-1785). He was a member of English Parliament and with a Charter, found the Colony of Georgia, in 1733.

During the 1800s the prime export of Savannah was cotton.

In 1864, on his march to the sea, William Tecumseh Sherman, entered the city of Savannah on Christmas day and found the city so beautiful that he gave it to President Abraham Lincoln as a present.

When Sherman approached Savannah, the city fathers met him and offered him Savannah, without a fight, if he would not destroy the city. This move made Savannah the jewel of history that it remains today.

Savannah has an incredible Historic District with stately homes adorned with wrought iron railings. The most remarkable feature of the city is the riverside park with the old cotton warehouses and cobble-stone streets.

Throughout Savannah there are park-like town squares, graced by stately oaks. One of the most notable is Chippewa Square with a bronze statue of Oglethorpe. It was this square that was featured in the movie, *Forest Gump*.

My research discovered a John Muir living in Savannah prior to 1867. John Muir, (1731-?), who's father James was a peruke maker lived in Savannah in the 1700s. (A peruke is a wig of the type worn from the 17th to the 19th century).

Other historic events were gleaned from the *Savannah Newspaper Digest,* of January 1, 1867 to December 31, 1867. It is available at the Georgia Historical Society, located on the corner of West Gaston and Whitaker streets in Savannah.

September 6, 1867: "Contrary to all the dismal forebodings of the confirmed pessimists, who sniff malarial danger in every breeze, Savannah has maintained her position as the healthiest city of her size in the union."

May 25, 1867: "The press paid a visit to the ice house of J. H. Gould".

August 31, 1867: "The ice question has become of serious interest".

October 4, 1867: Commodity prices were discussed; "Butter 25¢/lb, Candy 25¢/lb, Cheese 14¢ - 20¢/ lb, Fish 9¢/ lb, Plaster's hair $8.00/ cwt. And vinegar 50¢/ gal".

BONAVENTURE CEMETERY:

While John Muir waited in Savannah for his finances, he found refuge in Bonaventure Cemetery. He chose to dwell in the cemetery for safety reasons.

"There", thought I "is an ideal place for a penniless wanderer. There no superstitious prowling mischief maker dares venture for fear of haunting ghosts, while for me there will be God's rest and peace".
John Muir, October 9, 1867.

Bonaventure, three miles from Savannah, at the time, was reached by a white shell road. These came from middens of discarded shells of Oysters and Clams.

When I visited Bonaventure Cemetery, the receptionist at the visitor's center assumed that I, like many other visitors ahead of me, was looking for the "Bird Girl". He was referring to Sylvia Shaw Judson's, 1936 sculpture which resided in the cemetery. A photo of The "Bird Girl" appeared on the cover of the book, *Midnight in the Garden of Good and Evil,* written by John Berendt in 1994. The sculpture became so popular after the movie of the same name; it was moved, to preserve the dignity of the family plot, to the Telfair Academy of Arts and Sciences at 121, Bernard Street. When the receptionist learned that my interest was in John Muir's visit, the mood changed to enlightenment. He took me outside and showed me the location of the white shell road – now covered with asphalt. I was also directed to the 1867 period of Bonaventure where the moss draped oak trees still shaded the tombs.

Bonaventure Cemetery (1867 area), Savannah, Georgia

With the following statement, Muir discusses his greatest find at the Bonaventure Cemetery.

"The most conspicuous glory of Bonaventure is its noble avenue of live-oaks".
 John Muir, October 9, 1867.

Muir writes the following about the Eagles;

"Many Bald Eagles roost among the trees along the side of the marsh".

He then goes on to say,

"Bonaventure to me is one of the most impressive assemblages of animal and plant creatures I ever met".

As Muir resides at Bonaventure, during the lull in his travels, he reflects on death and dying.

"On no subject are our ideas more warped and pitiable than on death. Instead of the sympathy, the friendly union, of life and death so apparent in nature, we are taught that death is an accident, a deplorable punishment for the oldest sin, the arch-enemy of life, etc".

Muir continues with:

"But let children walk with nature, let them see the beautiful blendings and communions of death and life, their joyous inseparable unity, as taught in woods and meadows, plains and mountains and streams of our blessed star, and they will learn that death is stingless indeed, and as beautiful as life, and the grave has no victory, for it never fights. All is divine harmony".
John Muir, October, 1867.

Muir also reflects on the war, with the destruction of the forests as a type of metaphor.

"The traces of war are not only apparent on the broken fields, burnt fences, mills, and woods ruthlessly slaughtered, but also on the countances of the people".
John Muir, October, 1867.

NOTE: In 1898, Muir would again visit Bonaventure Cemetery, while on a trip to Florida.

Muir's money finally arrived in Savannah and after a lengthy ordeal of him trying to prove his identity he finally had funds to purchase food.

"Gladly I pocketed my money, and had not gone along the street more than a few rods before I met a very large negro woman with a tray of gingerbread, in which I immediately invested some of my new wealth, and walked rejoicingly, munching along the street, making no attempt to conceal the pleasure I had in eating. Then, still hunting for more food, I found a sort of eating-place in a market and had a large regular meal on top of the gingerbread! Thus my "marching through Georgia" terminated handsomely in a jubilee of bread".
John Muir, October, 1867.

"The same day on which the money arrived I took passage on the steam ship Sylvan Shore for Fernandina, Florida".
John Muir, October, 1867.

In 1867, travelers departing Savannah for Fernandina or St. Augustine had several choices of steamships that serviced this route; the *Dictator, Lizzy Baker* or *Sylvan Shore.*

Muir set out for Fernandina, Florida, no doubt following what is today known as the Intracoastal Waterway, whose waters are protected by barrier islands. During his trip along the Georgia coast, Muir writes;

"Altogether my half-day and night on board the steamer were pleasant".
John Muir, October 14, 1867.

I began my drive south on Interstate 95. After crossing the Florida state line at the St. Mary's River, I took U.S. 17 south to the town of Yulee, then Florida route A1A into Fernandina.

60

6

FLORIDA

"To-day, at last I reached Florida, the so-called "Land of Flowers".
John Muir, October 15, 1867.

On a map of 1690, Florida was named, *Presqu Isle de la Florida.*

FERNANDINA, FLORIDA:

"The steamer finds her way among the reedy islands like a duck, and I step on a rickety wharf. A few steps more take me to a rickety town, Fernandina".
John Muir, October 15, 1867.

Fernandina is located on Amelia Island. In 1736, James Edward Oglethorpe, Governor of Georgia, named the island "Amelia", after Princess Amelia Sophia Eleanor (1710-1786), the daughter of King George II (1683- 1760) of England.

Fernandina, now Fernandina Beach, was called a, "Festering Fleshpot", by President James Monroe (1758-1831), because of its association with pirates and smugglers. Today Fernandina is an up-scale community with an impressive historic district.

The Amelia Island Museum of History is located within the historic Nassau County Jail. The folks at the museum were quite helpful with my research.

Fernandina is located on Amelia Island which over time was the possession of several international owners, starting with: France from1562 to1565; Spain from1565 to1763; England from1763 to 1783; Spain from 1783 to1821; The Patriots of Amelia Island from 1812to1816 - <u>The Patriots of Amelia Island</u>; overthrew the Spanish but Spain regained control; Green Cross of Florida 1817 - <u>Green Cross of Florida</u>; Sir Gregor MacGregor seized the area in 1817 from Spain; Mexican Rebel Flag 1817 – <u>Mexican Rebel Flag</u>; Jared Irwin and Ruggles Hubbard with Pirate Luis Aury held Amelia "in trust, for Spain; America 1821-1861; Confederacy 1861-1868 and then the United States from1868 to the Present.

In Fernandina the historic marker near the railroad station, now housing the Chamber of Commerce discusses the trail of William Bartram, which reads:

"William Bartram Trail traced 1773-1777.
In 1774, William Bartram famed Colonial Naturalist visited Amelia Island and recorded the flora and fauna of this area".
The marker was erected by the Rose Garden Club, Fernandina Beach, Florida-in cooperation with the Federation of Garden Clubs, Inc. and the City of Fernandina Beach, Florida.

Fernandina was visited by members of what was known as, "High Society", the Vanderbilt's, DuPont's, and the Carnegie's. In 1867, Henry Morrison Flagler, (1830-1913), and John D. Rockefeller, (1839-1937), became partners and formed the Standard Oil Company, producing 10,000 barrels a day. Henry Flagler soon became one of the richest men in the world.

"I started to cross the state by a gap hewn for the locomotive, walking sometimes between the rails, stepping from tie to tie, or walking on the strip of sand at the sides, gazing into the mysterious forest, Nature's own".
John Muir, October 15, 1867.

The town of Fernandina was laid out by the Florida Railroad Company in 1855. It had a central park which was located between 11th and 13th streets. Many of the streets were paved with white shells that were gleaned from prehistoric mounds.

The Florida Railroad was built to transport goods across northern Florida rather than shipping them around the entire coastline of the state.

The following describes the building of the Florida Railroad:

"Fighting mosquitoes, sand gnats, wild animals and disgruntled settlers, the crews, composed of slaves and a small number of white laborers, hacked through the dense jungle growth and placed the rails, mile after mile through lonely desolate country. The first ten miles of the road took almost a year to build".[23]

The Florida Railroad was chartered in 1853, by David Yulee. "David Levy Yulee, (1810-1886), was one of Florida's foremost promoters and developers during the territorial and early periods. In 1821, he arrived in Florida from the West Indies with his father, Moses Elias Levy. [David Levy changed his name to Yulee and renounced Judaism and adopted Christianity]. His father, the first prominent Jew in the peninsula, acquired large landholdings in what became Alachua County. David entered politics of the new U.S. territory, became a delegate to the Constitutional Convention of 1838, territorial delegate to Congress in 1841, and when statehood came, U.S. Senator in 1845-51 and 1855-61. No one had worked harder to bring Florida into the Union, but he supported secession and served in the Confederate Congress, 1861-1865. His economic development activities were best represented by the cross-state Florida Railroad that he completed in 1861 from Cedar Key on the Gulf coast to Fernandina on the Atlantic. [Yulee was president of the Florida Railroad, with the construction completed by Joseph Finegan]. The family name perpetuated in Levy County and the town of Yulee".[24]

While I was in Fernandina I visited Fort Clinch, (1847-present), where I saw an armadillo stumbling about. One might wonder what Muir thought of this strange creature.

Florida House Inn, circa 1857: Fernandina, Florida

    On my many trips to Fernandina I spent several nights at the Florida House Inn which is reported to be Florida's oldest hotel. It was built by the railroad in 1857. The present owners are Diane and Joe Warwick. I was honored when he asked me to join him in a few songs for his dining patrons.

    During my stay I learned from Joe Warwick that the Doug Muir family lived in Fernandina. During my conversation with Doug Muir I found that he was reportedly related to John Muir, the naturalist. Doug said that his grandfather moved from Scotland to Clifton, New Jersey in the late 1890s. Doug's father David Allen Muir was born in 1915 and his mother in 1925. Doug said that he ended up in Fernandina by life's circumstance rather than because John Muir passed through in 1867.

    In front of the Florida House Inn there is a marker remembering Jose' Marti (1853-1895). It reads as follows:

    "Cuban patriot and poet, champion of liberty and of respect for human dignity, lived here in February 1893 during his struggle for the independence of his country (Cuba). Fernandina Beach, January 28, 1990". It was donated by; Latin American Club of Jacksonville and the Spanish-American Cultural Association of Jacksonville.

John Muir left Fernandina and Amelia Island via the Florida Railroad. As he begins his trek across Florida he makes the following statement:

"I thank the Lord with all my heart for his goodness in granting me admission to this magnificent realm".
John Muir, October 15, 1867.

I said something similar while visiting Inyo Craters in the Sierra Nevada Mountains. I walked away from one of the craters and climbed a hill to take a photograph of the crater that I just left, and as I turned, In front of me, just over the trees, was the majestic Mammoth Mountain, with its spectacular beauty. I said; "Thank you God for letting me see this".

Had Muir made his trip today, he would see, to the south, the cooling towers of the Jacksonville Power Station.

As Muir began to cross Florida the first town that he would have passed through was Harts Road, which was later changed to Yulee in 1893.

Today in Yulee there is an ecological park located along the original Florida Railroad. A sign at the entrance reads;

"John Muir Ecological Park; The John Muir ecological park is being constructed for the citizens of Nassau County by the Nassau County Board of Commissioners as a settlement of an enforcement action brought against Nassau County by the Department of Environmental Protection".

Mary Lou Tucker of Yulee, who is president of the Yulee Historical Council Incorporated, said that the "enforcement action" was from a landfill violation and John Muir was used to satisfy the ecological requirement of the settlement.

As Muir continued his walk he would pass through the towns of; Callahan Station, St. Mary's Station then Baldwin. Baldwin was the junction point of the Florida Railroad and the Atlantic and Gulf Central Railroad, from Jacksonville. It was a distribution station with warehouses; these were burned in 1864. That same year, the rails were torn up from Fernandina to Baldwin, to build a rail line from Baldwin, North into Georgia. It opened in 1865, too late to help the Confederacy.

> *"Arrived at a place on the margin of a stagnant pool where an alligator had been rolling and sunning himself".*
> John Muir, October 16, 1867.

One cannot talk about the swamps of Florida without including the alligator. The American alligator, *Alligator mississipensis,* can be from six feet to twenty feet in length. They inhabit the coastal lowland swamps and waterways from North Carolina to Texas and are throughout the entire state of Florida.

The American Crocodile, *Crocodylus acutus,* and reportedly the Spectacled Caiman, *Caiman crocodiles,* are also found in Florida but are somewhat restricted to the area of the Everglades.

This story about alligators brings to mind my kayaking trip through Georgia's Okefenokee Swamp. There was such an abundance of alligators that I was never out of sight of them. They appeared in lengths from four feet, to the twenty foot monster that lay on a log, sunning itself. As I paddled along they cruised beside me, at times, only four feet away. It is little wonder that the sign at the put-in read, "NO SWIMMING-NO PETS". As I was returning from my paddle, I thought that I would get a better look at the twenty foot sun bathing 'gator', but when I reached the log on which it was sunning, it was gone-he was under water; somewhere.

As Muir continued on his trip across Florida, he would pass the town of Trail Ridge Station, where the railroad crosses a ridge and an old Indian trail. Trail Ridge Station would later be called Highland.

The next town along Muir's route is Starke Station. Then at Waldo Station, another railroad line extends southward.

Near Gainesville, Florida, Muir would again cross the trail of the Quaker botanists, the Bartrams, who made two visits there in 1774.

As I left Fernandina I followed Muir along route 200 to coastal route A1A, passing through Yulee and on to Callahan. From Callahan I took U.S. 301 south through Baldwin and Highland; stopping for the night in the town of Starke. In the middle of the night, I was awakened by the sound of a train whistle. When Muir walked the Florida Railroad it was no doubt the train whistle that cut through nature's silence, a nature that he much enjoyed. Leaving Stark in the morning, I continued along U.S. 301 to Waldo where I turned south-west onto route 24 which I then followed to Gainesville.

GAINESVILLE, FLORIDA:

"Reached Gainesville late in the night".
"Gainesville is rather attractive-an oasis in the desert, compared with other villages. It gets its life from the few plantations located about it on dry ground that rises island-like a few feet above the swamps. Obtained food and lodging at a sort of tavern".
John Muir, October 18, 1867.

On September 6, 1853, the seat of Alachua County was moved from Newmansville to Gainesville because Gainesville was situated on the proposed route of the Florida Railroad. In 1856, a two story wooden Court House was built, on piers, to provide a shaded space for animals.

During the year of Muir's visit, 1867, a prominent businessman and merchant, Alexander Matheson, built his house in Gainesville, which is now a history center.

During the Civil War, David Yulee moved his railroad office to Gainesville.

After the Civil War ended, schools for freedmen began to be established in various parts of the south. Conditions and facilities in these schools were poor to non-existent. The East Florida Seminary moved to Gainesville in 1866 and merged with Gainesville Academy.

In an advertisement for the East Florida Seminary the tuition and fees were discussed:

"County appointees pay no tuition, all other students pay for each term of nineteen weeks tuition, as follows:

For English Course Proper	$10.00
For Book keeping	$ 5.00
For lessons in rudiments of vocal music, 18 weeks, two lessons per week	$ 4.00
Books for Class F, cost about	$ 4.00

Board in good families cost from $12.00 to $15.00 per calendar month. Washing $1.00 per month.[25]

Life in Florida, around the time of Muir's visit, is described in the following:

"The first sewing machine was brought to St. Augustine about 1865. Cook stoves were received, at first with much suspicion for fear that they would explode and it took many years to popularize friction matches to kindle a fire and to displace the old flint and steel. Whale oil lamps and tallow candles made at home, (as well as soap), enabled them to read the few papers that, from time to time, drifted in with news of the outside world. Mail's were few and far between and very irregular and not until the early 'nineties' did steam permanently take the place of wind, on the inland waterways of Florida".[26]

I continued following Muir's trail out of Gainesville on route 24 to the town of Archer.

Although the town of Archer is not included in Muir's published account, it is worth mentioning.

In 1850, Archer was once called Deer Hammock then Darden's Hammock. In 1858 it was named Archer after James T. Archer, Florida's first Secretary of State.

The first train stopped in Archer in 1859.

It was in Archer that Muir, on a return visit to Florida in 1898, found Mrs. Hodgson, who nursed him during his bout with Malaria while in Cedar Key Florida in 1867. On November 21, 1898, Muir described his meeting with Mrs. Hodgson in a letter to his wife Louie, [Louisa Wanda Strentzel Muir]:

"I asked her if she knew me. She answered no, and asked my name. I said Muir. *"John Muir"?* She almost screamed. *"My*

California John Muir? My California John"? I said, "Why yes. I promised to come back and visit you in about twenty-five years, and though a little late I've come".[27]

After visiting in Archer I continued south-west on route 24 toward Otter Creek and Cedar Key. [Archer was coincidently the location of the museum and factory of the late famed <u>archer</u> Fred Bear].

As Muir traveled west, near the town of Otter Creek he would have again crossed the trail of Hernando De Soto who, on his march north, first crossed the Withlacoochee River and then Otter Creek.

With the following journal entry Muir touches on his loneliness:

"Slept in the barrens at the side of a log. Suffered from cold and was drenched with dew. What a comfort a companion would be in the dark loneliness of such nights! Did not dare to make a fire for fear of discovery by robber Negroes, who, I was warned, would kill a man for a dollar or two".
John Muir, October 19, 1867.

About nine miles East of Cedar Key there are two towns which Muir no doubt passed through, but do not exist today. These are the towns of Rosewood and the nearby town of Sumner.

Rosewood was surveyed in 1847 and was named for the Red Cedar trees, which were abundant in the area. Rosewood, a Negro community was never incorporated.

The town of Rosewood came to a gruesome end in January of 1923 when a mob of racists started shooting residents at Sumner then moved to Rosewood. On January 4th several people, both black and white were killed and the residents of Rosewood fled into the nearby swamps, while a black church and homes were burned. On January 6th a train took the remaining residents to Archer and Gainesville. Then on January 7th the remaining structures of Rosewood were burned. On February 15th, 1923 a Florida Grand Jury determined that there was "insufficient evidence" to prosecute anyone for the Rosewood massacre.

In 1994, the Florida Legislature passed the *Rosewood Claims Bill,* giving nine of the Rosewood survivors, $150,000 each.

CEDAR KEY, FLORIDA:

"I beheld the Gulf of Mexico stretching away unbounded, except by the sky".
"But now at the seaside I was in difficulty. I had reached a point that I could not ford, and Cedar Keys had an empty harbor".
John Muir, October 23, 1867.

Note: There are no longer any <u>dated</u> journal entries after Muir reaches Cedar Key on October 23, 1867.

At the State Museum at Cedar Key, which is located just off Hodgson Drive, there is a historic marker that Highlights John Muir's 1867 walk and reads as follows:

John Muir at Cedar Key
John Muir, noted naturalist and conservation leader spent several months in Florida in 1867. He arrived at Cedar Key in October, seven weeks after setting out, from Indiana on a "thousand mile walk to the Gulf". Muir's journal account of his adventure, which was published in 1916, two years after his death includes interesting glimpses of the quality of life in the post-Civil War South. "The traces of war". He wrote, "Are not only apparent on the broken fields, mills, and woods ruthlessly slaughtered, but also on the countenances of the people". Florida deeply impressed the twenty-nine year old Muir. He remembered the "watery and vine-tied ", land where, "the streams are still young", which he had seen and sampled on his way from Fernandina. It was while recovering from a bout with malaria in Cedar Key that Muir first expressed his belief that nature was valuable for its own sake, not only because it was useful for man. This principle guided John Muir throughout his life. In early 1868, he left Cedar Key and eventually settled in California where he helped establish Yosemite National Park and

in 1892 the Sierra Club which became one of our nation's best known environmental organizations

   The marker was sponsored by the Florida Chapter of the Sierra Club, in cooperation with the Department of State, 1983.

   From 1770 to 1772, Cedar Key was mapped by Bernard Romans (1720-1784). Romans, born in the Netherlands, was appointed Deputy Surveyor for Georgia in 1766. In this role he charted both the east and west coast of Florida. In 1775, he published, *A Concise Natural History of East and West Florida.* The work included maps which were engraved by Paul Revere, (1735-1818).
   The area around Cedar Key became an important resource in the mid 1850s when Eberhard Faber (1822-1879), purchased, at fifty cents an acre, several hundred acres containing Cedar trees that he would use in his world wide pencil business.
   The Suwannee Lumber Company built the first saw mill at Cedar Key in 1858. There would eventually be thirteen sawmills at Cedar Key.
   Cedar trees were located along the local rivers where they were trimmed and cut into twelve foot pieces and floated down stream. The river most important to Cedar Key was the Suwannee.
   The Suwannee River was also immortalized by song writer Stephen Collins Foster who, when searching for a river that would fit the lyrics better than the Pedee River of North Carolina, picked the Suwannee from an atlas; Foster was never near the Suwannee. Foster shortened the name then wrote, "Way down upon the Swanee ribber". The song was *Old Folks at Home,* which Foster published on October 1, 1851. As noted earlier, the song, depicting life along the Suwannee River, was adopted as Florida's state song in 1935.
   Cedar Key, on the Gulf of Mexico, developed into an important city for shipping lumber. Yulee's Florida Railroad across the state to Fernandina made Cedar Key more popular for shipping goods from the Gulf coast, especially from New Orleans.
   This transportation hub became very important during the American Civil War. It was used by the Confederacy until January

15, 1862, when union troops took control of Cedar Key then took over Fernandina on March 3, 1862. When Federal troops took over Cedar Key, they destroyed the salt works. Salt, a very important resource of the period, was produced by boiling down sea water in large sheet-iron kettles. One surviving kettle is on display at the Cedar Key State Museum.

Sheet-Iron Salt Kettle: Cedar Key State Museum, Florida

After the war, the industrial conditions improved at Cedar Key. The timber business resumed and the mills continued production. This prosperity lasted until the timber resource became exhausted and a catastrophic hurricane hit Cedar Key in September of 1896 which destroyed the mills beyond repair.

While Muir was awaiting a ship to take him to New Orleans, then to points south, he was offered a job at a saw mill in Cedar Key partially owned by Richard W.B. Hodgson who originally came from Georgia during the lumber boon in the late 1850s.

A day after Muir's arrival at Cedar Key he fell ill with a malaria fever and was cared for by Hodgson's wife, Sarah A Hodgson.

Malaria is an infection of Plasmodium obtained from the blood of infected persons carried by the *Anopheles* mosquito. Muir's trip along the Savannah River and across Florida surely exposed him to this disease. The incubation period for malaria is between six to fourteen days making Muir's contact with the disease from October 10th to October 18th. In his journal he discussed an account of being exposed to malaria.

"Came to a hut about noon, and being weary and hungry, I asked if I could have dinner. After serious consultation I was told to wait, that dinner would soon be ready. I saw only the man and his wife. If they had children, they may have been hidden in the weeds on account of nakedness. Both were suffering from malarial fever, and were very dirty. But they did not appear to have any realizing sense of discomfort from either the one or the other of these misfortunes".
John Muir, October 19, 1867.

Ironically, in June of 1867, a similar mosquito borne disease, Yellow Fever, broke out at Fort Jefferson on the Dry Tortugas, in the Florida Keys. Upon the death of Joseph Sim Smith the forts only doctor, a prisoner and doctor, named Samuel Alexander Mudd (1833-1883), a medical school class-mate of Smiths took over Smiths duties. The care that Mudd provided the prisoners resulted in his unconditional pardon by President Andrew Johnson in 1869. Dr. Samuel Mudd was imprisoned at Fort Jefferson as a co-conspirator in the Lincoln assassination for setting the broken leg of John Wilkes Booth.

With the following statement, Muir discusses his ailments and treatments.

"Through quinine and calomel – in sorry abundance – with milder medicines, my malarial fever became typhoid. I had night sweats, and my legs became like posts of the temper and consistency of clay on account of dropsy".
John Muir, Cedar Key, 1867.

Typhoid is a communicable disease with fever, diarrhea, prostration, headache and intestinal inflammation caused by the bacterium *Salmonella typhosa*.

Muir was being treated with two commonly used medicines of the time, Calomel and Quinine. Calomel, or Mercurous Chloride, is used as a purgative and fungicide. Quinine is a bitter crystalline alkaloid, made from cinchona bark, which comes from tropical evergreen trees of the Amazonian slopes of the Andes. It is used as a febrifuge, (an antipyretic or fever reducer), antimalorial treatment.

As Muir convalesced he gained strength enough to continue his botanizing and began sailing from key to key in a borrowed skiff. He observed plants, birds and the other adjoining keys and wrote eloquently about them.

Bade, in his introduction to, *A Thousand Mile Walk to the Gulf,* discusses a letter that Muir wrote, dated November 8, 1867, describing his condition. "Just creeping about getting plants and strength after my fever".

In one account, Muir touches on the Creator and, "handfuls of insignificant things".

"With such views of the Creator it is, of course, not surprising that erroneous views should be entertained of the creation. To such properly trimmed people, the sheep, for example, is an easy problem-food and clothing, "for us", eating grass and daisies white by divine appointment for this predestined purpose, on perceiving the demand for wool that would be occasioned by the eating of the apple in the Garden of Eden.

In the same pleasant plan, whales are storehouses of oil for us, to help out the stars in lighting our dark ways until the discovery of the Pennsylvania oil wells, [Colonel Edwin L. Drake struck oil in Titusville, Pennsylvania on August 28, 1859]. Among plants, hemp, to say nothing of the cereals, is a case of evident destination for ships rigging, wrapping packages and hanging the wicked. Cotton is another plain case of clothing. Iron was made for hammers and ploughs, and lead for bullets; all intended for us. And so of other small handfuls of insignificant things".

John Muir, Cedar Key, 1867.

During his time on Cedar Key, Muir writes of the relationship with God and nature and his understanding of this union. His thousand mile walk was the true birth of his future way of life. Although he had gone on many botanizing trips in the past, this one was sure to shape his future. He would incorporate his findings and hardships, and to a greater degree his solitude and time for reflection, into his study and teaching of nature. Perhaps if Muir would have made his walk sooner, there would still be the great Cedar trees in Florida.

Muir's illness made it difficult for him to follow his aspirations to South America like an earlier naturalist; Fredrich Heinrich Alexander, Baron von Humboldt (1769-1859).

Muir walked to the Gulf of Mexico in a time when technology was just beginning. For, if he stood on the dock at Cedar Key today, he would see the cooling towers of the Crystal River Nuclear Power Station on the southern horizon.

Cedar Key is continuously changing. When gill nets were banned for fishing in 1995, the area became an aquaculture leader in Hard Clam production. Nutrients from the Suwannee River are a positive attribute that enhances the rapid growth of the clam 'seedlings'.

On one clear morning in January 1868, Muir spotted a schooner in the port at Cedar Key; it was the *Island Belle*.

In November 1861 the *Island Belle* was captured by the *U.S.S. Augusta* while she was a blockade runner along with another ship, the *Cheshire*, off the coast of Charleston, South Carolina.

Muir booked passage aboard the *Island Belle* for twenty-five dollars as she was ready to sail for Cuba with a load of lumber.

On a January day in 1868, Muir left Cedar Key and the United States, temporarily, to continue on his life's journey. His fledgling years of botanizing and his thousand mile walk to the Gulf, prepared him for the naturalist that he was to become.

"The little craft was quickly trimmed and snugged, her inviting sails spread open, and away she dashed to her ocean home like an exalting war-horse to the battle. Islet after islet speedily grew dim and sank beneath the horizon. Deeper became the blue of the water, and in a few hours all of Florida vanished".

John Muir, January 1868. The Gulf of Mexico

ENDNOTES

Chapter 1 Indianna

[1] John Muir. A Thousand Mile Walk to the Gulf.. Houghton Mifflin Company. New York. 1916. 17.
[2] Joseph Ray, M.D. Practical Arithmetic, Van Antwerp Bragg & Co. Cincinnati Ohio. 1857. 71.
[3] U.S. Supreme Court, Louisville and Jeffersonville Ferry Company vs. Commonwealth of Kentucky 188 US 385 (1903) Argued January 17, 1902 to recover taxes for the year 1894

Chapter 3 Tennessee

[4] One who has seen it.. Other Fools and Their Doings, or life Among the Freemen. J.S. Ogilvie and Company. New York. 1880. 148-9
[5] The Heritage of Morgan County, Tennessee 1817-1999. pg19. (reprint)
[6] Sarah Sands. History of Monroe County Tennessee, Volume I, part 2.1982.227
[7] Excerpts from; Federal Endangered Species Act: Selected Cases. Tennessee Valley Authority v. Hill, 437 U.S. 153 (1978) "The Snail Darter Case".
[8] Jared Diamond. Guns Germs and Steel. W.W. Norton & Company. New York-London, 1999. 211.
[9] Eric Burkhart. Keystone WILD Notes –Summer, 2005, Picked to Death,.
[10] John Mack Faragher.Daniel Boone. Henry Holt and Company, New York. 1992. 260-61.

Chapter 5 Georgia

[11] Sybil Wood McRay. This'N-That: History of Hall County Georgia. Peoples Printing Service. 1973. 9.
[12] James Dorsey. The History of Hall County, Georgia, Vol. I 1818-1900. Magnolia Press. Georgia.1991. 168.
[13] The Daily Times, Gainesville Georgia, Sunday, March 23, 1969, Section 2-E.
[14] James K. Reap. Athens, A Pictorial History. Donning Co. Publishers. Virginia. 1958. 46.
[15] In the Preface to No. 14.
[16] Public Television Documentary. The Amazing Story of Kudzu. University of Alabama Center for Public Television and Radio.
[17] Mrs. W.C. Mc Commons and Miss Clara Stovall. History of McDuffie County, Georgia. Boyd Publishing Co. Georgia. 1988. 83.

[18] Pearl Baker. A Handbook of History, Mc Duffie County, Georgia 1870-1970, , Progress News Publishing Company, (no date given). 24-25.
[19] Augusta Bicentennial Publications Pageant Book. 30.
[20] Julia Faye Smith. The Civil War Childhood of a President. Russell House Publications. Georgia. 1996. 40.
[21] Edward J. Cashin. The Story of Augusta. The Reprint Company Publishers. South Carolina. 1996.3
[22] The Place We Call Home. The Augusta Chronicle 1997, The Augusta Chronicle, Augusta, Georgia. 3.

Chapter 6 Florida

[23] Celeste H Kavanaugh. David Levy Yulee, a man and his vision. Amelia Island Museum of History. 1992. 22.
[24] Michael Gannon. Florida, A short History. University Press of Florida. Gainesville, Florida. 1993. 38.
[25] C.H. Webber. Eden of the South. Love and Aldens Publication Department. New York. 1883. 110.
[26] Frederick W. Dau. Florida, Old and New. G.P. Putnam's Sons. New York-London. 1934. 234-235.
[27] Fredric Turner. John Muir, Rediscovering America, Perseus Publishing, Cambridge Massachusetts. 1985. 315.

INDEX:

A
Abbe, Cleveland, 22
Agassiz, Jean Louis
    Rodolphe, 30
Alachua County, FL, 63, 67
Alligator mississipensis, 66
Alligator, American, 66
Amazon River, 12
Amelia Island, 61, 62, 65
Amelia Island Museum of
    History, 61
Amelia Sophia Eleanor, 61
American Philosophical
    Society, 52
Anopheles (mosquito), 72
Antebellum, 34
Appalachian Trail, 45
Appomattox, 32
Archer, FL, 68, 69
Archer, James T, 68
Armadillo, 63
Athens, GA, 47, 48
Atlanta Constitution, 44
Atlantic and Gulf Central
    Railroad, 65
Audubon, John James, 17
Augusta, GA, 49-53, 55
Augusta Canal, 51
Aury, Luis, 62

B
Bade, William Fredric, 7, 16,
    40

Bailey, Robert, 8, 35

Baker, (Senator-TN.)
    Howard, 38
Bamboo, 48
Bardstown, KY, 17, 18
Bardstown Road, 17, 25
Barren Co. KY, 26
Barron, Debby, 8
Bartram, John, 52, 53
Bartram, William, 17, 52, 53,
    62, 66
Bear, Fred, 69
Bell, William, 25
Bells Tavern, 25
    Ruins, **26**
Bird Girl, 57
Black Fish, (Shawnee Chief),
    7
Blair, James, 44
Blairsville, GA, 43-45
Blodgell, Foster, 51
Boone, Daniel, 7, 20, 41
Boone, Rebecca, 41
Boone, William P, 20
Booth, John Wilkes, 73
Bonaventure Cemetery, 7,
    57-60
Botanical Textbook, (Gray),
    30
Brent, John, 57
Brewstertown, TN, 32
Brown-Pusey House, 21, **22**
Brownlow, (Governor, TN)
    William G, 31
Burke, Samuel, 28
Burkesville, KY, 27, 28
Burkesville-Glasgow Road,
    26, 27
Butler, B.F, 42

Butler, Fort, 42, 43
Byrd, J. H, 34

C
Caiman crocodiles, 66
Caiman Spectacled, 66
California, 6, 8, 12
Callahan, FL, 66
Canada, 11
Carpetbaggers, 33
Cashin, Edwin, 52
Cave City, KY, 23
Cedar Key, FL, 6, 8, 63, 69-72, 75, 76
Cedar Key Museum, 8
Celsius Temperature Scale, 31
Centennial Exposition in Philadelphia, PA, 48
Charleston, SC, 54
Chattahoochee River, 46
Chattahoochee National Forest, 44, 45
Cherokee, 40, 43
Cherokee Co. NC, 42
Cherokee Indians, 42
Cherokee Indian Reservation, 42
Cherokee National Forest, 41
China, 40
Chippewa Square, Savannah GA, 56
Church-Waddel-Brumby House, 48
Civil War, 9, 11, 23, 28, 32, 42, 47, 48, 51, 67, 70, 71
Clarke Co. GA, 47

Clark, William, 53
Class Book of Botany, (Wood), 29, 30
Clemens, John M, 31
Clemens, Samuel, (Mark Twain), 31
Collins, Floyd, 24
Collinson, Peter, 52
Columbus, Christopher, 39
Concise Natural History of East and West Florida, 71
Confederacy, 29, 44, 62, 65, 71
Confederate Congress, 63
Confederate States, 32
Crocodile, American, 66
Crocodylus acutus, 66
Crotalus borridus, 47
Crystal River Nuclear Power Station, 75
Cuba, 8, 12, 75
Cumberland Co. KY, 28
Cumberland River, 28
Custer, George Armstrong, 21

D
Darwin, Charles, 30
Davis, Jefferson, 48, 49
Department of Environmental Protection, 65
Department of the Interior, 39
De Soto, Hernando, 39, 54, 69
Dahlonega, GA, 42
Dictator, 60

Domino, (Michael Muir's Horse) 6
Drake, Col. Edwin L, 74
Dry Tortugas, 73
Dunbar, Scotland, 11
Duncan, John, (Congressman, TN), 38

E
Eagles, Bald, 59
Earl, John, 8
East Florida Seminary, 67, 68
Edison, Thomas, 8
Elements of Botany, (Gray), 30
Elgin Botanical Garden, 52
Elgin, TN, 33
Elizabethtown, KY, 20
Endangered Species Act, 38
England, 62
Eocene Epoch, 54
Eupaorium perfoliatum, 20
Everglades, 66

F
Faber, Eberhard, 71
Federal Hill, 19
Fentress Co. TN, 31
Fentress, James, 31
Fernandina, FL, 60-66, 70, 71
Fernandina Beach, FL, 61, 64
Field, Forest and Garden Botany, 30
Finegan, Joseph, 63
First Lesson in Botany, (Wood), 30
Flagler, Henry Morrison, 62

Florida, 6, 44, 53, 60, 61, 63, 66, 70, 72
Florida House Inn, **64**
Florida Railroad, 63, 65, 67, 71
Florida State Museum, Cedar Key, 6-8, 70, 72
Forest Gump, 56
Fort Jefferson, 73
Fort Knox Military Reservation, 18
Fort Sumter, SC, 32
Foster, Stephen Collins, 19, 71
Franklin, Benjamin, 52, 54
Fraser, John, 54
    Fir, 54
    Magnolia, 54
Frog Pond, GA, 49

G
Gainesville, FL, 66, 67, 69
Gainesville Academy, 67
Gainesville, GA, 46, 47
Georgia, 43-45, 47, 50, 60, 72
Georgia Historical Society, 56
Georgia Regional Library, Augusta, 8
Georgia University, Athens, 47
George II, England, 61
George III, England, 52
Gideon Morgan House, 35, **36**
Ginseng "sang", 40, 41
Glasgow, KY, 26

Glasgow Junction, KY, 24, 25
Goff, Cindy, 6
Gould, J.H, 57
Grass- Cogon, 48
Gray, Asa, 30, 52
Great Falls of the Ohio, 14, 16
Greeley, Horace, 49
Green Cross of Florida, 62
Gulf of Mexico, 6, 70, 76

H
Hall Co. GA, 46
Hardy, Oliver Norvell Jr, 50
Harlem, GA, 50
Harris, Joel Chandler, 44
Harshaw Chapel, 43
Harts Road, 65
Hawkins, Col. Benjamin, 45
Hetch Hetchy Valley, 39, 51
Hiawassee, 39
Hiawassee Lake, 42
Hiawassee River, 41, 42
Hickory Level, GA, 49
Highland, FL, 66
Hodgson, Richard W.B, 72
Hodgson, Sarah A, 68, 72
Holly, 43
Horse Cave, 23
Hosack, Dr. David, 52
Hubbard, Ruggles, 62
Humbolt, Alexander, Freiherr von, 12, 75
Huntersville, NC, 42
Huntington, NC, 42
Hutchings, James Mason, 11
Hyperion, Steamboat, 14

I
Imperata cylinrica, 48
Indiana, 11, 12
Indianapolis, IN, 11, 12, 13
Intracoastal Waterway, 60
Inyo Craters, 65
Irwin, Jared, 62
Irwinsville, GA, 48
Island Belle, 75

J
Jackson, Andrew, 34
Jacksonville Power Station, 65
Jamestown, TN, 31, 33
Jay, Charles, 11
Jefferson, Thomas, 13, 53
Jeffersonville, IN, 13, 14
Jeffersonville, IN, (Train Station), **14**
Johnson, Andrew, 73

K
Kefauver, Estes, 38
Kentucky, 6, 16, 17, 28, 48
Kentucky Knobs, 18
   Bolton, 18
   Orms, 18
   Stark, 18
Kingessing, PA, 52, 54
Kingston, TN, 34
Knox, William, 36
Knoxville-Nashville Turnpike, 34
Kudzu, 7, 48

L
Langston, John, 49

Laurel and Hardy, 50
Laurel, Stan, (Arthur
    Stanley), 50
Lee, Robert Edward, 32
Levy Co. FL, 63
Levy, Moses Elias, 63
Lincoln,
    Abraham, 20, 28, 56
    Nancy Hanks, 20, 21
    Thomas, 20, 21, 28
Linnaean Taxonomy, 30
Linnaeus, Carolus, 30
Linne, Carl von, 30
Lizzy Baker, 60
Lewis, Meriwether, 53
Louis XVI, France, 16, 54
Louisville, KY, 6, 15, 16, 28
Louisville and Jeffersonville
    Ferry Co, 15
Louisville-Nashville Pike, 25
Loyal Georgian, 51
    Weekly, 51

M
Mac Gregor, Sir George, 62
Madisonville, TN, 37, 38, 40, 51
Malaria, 8, 72, 73
Male-Female Symbols, 31
Mammoth Cave, 23, 24
Mammoth Cave National
    Park, 23, 24
Mammoth Mountain, 65
Marrowbone Creek, 28
Marti, Jose, 64
Matheson, Alexander, 67
Mc Lean, Wilmer, 32

Mexican Rebel Flag, 62
Michaux, Andre, 54
Midnight in the Garden of
    Good and Evil, 57
Millen, GA, 55
Mississippi River, 39
Monroe, Fort, (Fortress), 49
Monroe, James, 61
Montgomery, TN, 33, 34
Morgan Co. TN, 34
Mt. Katahdin, ME, 45
Mudd, Samuel Alexander, 73
Muir Doug, 64
Muir, John, (1731), 56
Muir, John
    Alligator, 66
    Birth, 11
    Blue Ridge, 45
    Bonaventure
        Cemetery, 57-60
    California, 12
    Camp Butler, 43
    Canada, 11
    Carriage Factory, 11
    Civil War, 59
    Death of, 12, 39
    On Death and Dying, 59
    Earth Planet
        Universe, 13
    Eye Injury, 12
    Fernandina, 61
    Florida-leaving, 76
    Florida Railroad, 62
    Forty miles a day, 50
    Gainesville, FL, 67
    Gold Mines, 40
    Gray in Yosemite, 30

Muir, John, (continued)
    Gulf of Mexico, 70
    Harvard invitation, 30
    Hetch Hetchy, 39
    Highway, 26
    Mrs. Hodgson meeting, (1898), 68, 69
    Indianapolis, IN, 11
    Leaving, 13
    Insignificant things, 74
    Island Bell, 75
    Interests, 31
    Kentucky, 28
    Kentucky Oaks, 17
    Loneliness, 69
    Lonesome and poor, 56
    Louisville, KY, 16
    Love for Nature, 12
    Malaria-exposure, 73
    Malaria-fever, 72
    Malaria-medication, 73, 74
    Mammoth Cave, 24
    Map, 16
    Men on horseback, 33
    Money arrives, 60
    Mount Yonah, 45
    Mr. Munford, 23
    Old Kentucky Home, 17
    Plant Collection, 34
    Plantation workers, 47
    Possessions, 13
    Public Resolution, 27

Muir, John, (continued)
    Rattlesnakes, 46, 47
    Rediscovering America, 11
    Robbers-fear of, 69
    Sang, ginseng, 40
    Savannah River, 52, 55
    Sawmill, Yosemite, 12
    Sylvan Shore, 60
    University Wisconsin, 11
    Water Oaks, 46
Muir Ecological Park, Yulee, FL, 65
Muir, Helen, (daughter), 7
Muir Highway, 26
Muir's longest walk, 8
Muir, Louisa Wanda Strentzel, Louie, 68
Muir, Michael, 6
Muir, Wanda, (daughter), 7
Munfordville, KY, 23
Murphey, Archibald D, 42
Murphy, NC, 41, 42
My Old Kentucky Home Goodnight, 19, 20

N
Nassau Co. FL, 65
Nassau Co. FL, Jail, 61
Nathanalia National Forest, 41
National Park Service, 45
Neese, Charles, 8
New York City, 8
Nobel, Alfred, 8

North Carolina, 32, 40-42

O
Oak, Black, 53
Oak Trees, KY, 17
Oaks of North America, 54
Oaks, Water, 46
Oglethorpe, James Edward, 56, 61
Ohio River, 14
Okefenokee Swamp, 66
Old Folks at Home, 71
Old Kentucky Home, 17-20
Old Kentucky Home, Goodnight, 19
Origin of Species, (Darwin), 30
Osgood and Smith, 11
Ostrea Georgiana, 54
Otter Creek, 69

P
Pall Mall, 29, 31
Panax quinquefolius, (ginseng), 40
Pangaea, 30
Paradise Lost, (Milton), 13
Pardo, Juan, 39
Park City, 24, 25
Patriots of Amelia Island, 62
Pearson, Jacob, 36
Pedee River, NC, 71
Philadelphia, PA, 52
Philadelphia, TN, 36, **37**
Philippe, Louis, France (Duke of Orleans), 36
Pizarro, Gonzalo, 12
Plasmodium, 72

Plate Tectonics, 30
Polk Co. TN, 41
Pope, General John, 44
Portland Canal, 16
Pueraria montania, (Kudzu), 48

R
Reconstruction, 29, 32, 33, 44
Rattlesnake, Timber, 47
Redwoods, 46
Revere, Paul, 71
Rise and Fall of the Confederate Government,(Davis), 49
Rix, Peggy, 8
Roan Co. TN, 35
Roan Co. Courthouse, **35**
Roan Co. Heritage Commission, 8, 35
Roan Co. Museum of History, 34
Rockefeller, John D, 62
Rolling Fork, 18
Romans, Bernard, 71
Rosewood, FL, 69
Rosewood Claims Bill, 70
Rowan, (Judge) John, 19

S
Salmonella typhosa, 74
Salt River, 17
Savannah, GA, 7, 44, 50, 51, 53, 56, 57
Savannah Newspaper Digest, 56

Savannah River, 49, 52-55, 72
Scallywags, 33
Schuylkill River, PA, 52
Scott, John L, 34
Scott, (General) Winfield, 42
Sequoias, 46
Sheet-iron Salt Kettle, **72**
Shell Bluff, GA, 54
Sheltowee, 7
Sherman, William Tecumseh, 47, 51, 56
Shermantowns, 47
Sierra Club, 7, 12, 71
Sierra Nevada Mountains, 12, 65
Slashes, the, GA, 49
Smith, Joseph Sim, 73
Snail Darter, (Perch), 38, 39
South America, 12
Spain, 62
Springer Mountain, GA, 45
Standard Oil Co. 62
Starke Station, FL, 66
Staunton, VA, 51
Stonewall, (horse breed), 6
Story of Augusta, (Cashin), 52
Stowe, Harriet Beecher, 19
Sumner, FL, 69
Suwannee Lumber Co. 71
Suwannee River, 71, 75
Sweetwater, TN, 37
Sylvan Shore, 60
System Naturae, 31

T
Tales of Uncle Remus, 44

Taylor, Frank B, 30
Telfair Academy of Arts and Sciences, 58
Tellico, TN, 38
Tellico Dam, 38
Tellico Lake, 38
Tellico Plains, 41
Tennessee, 28, 29
Tennessee River, Little, 38, 39
Tennessee Valley Authority, 38
Theory of Natural Selection, (Darwin), 30
Thompson, GA, 48-50
Thompson, GA, Train Station, **50**
Thousand Mile Walk to the Gulf, 6-8, 11, 16, 28, 40, 74
Three Forks, 25
Time Zone, 22, 32
Tobacco, 28
Travels, 53
Trail Ridge Station, FL, 66
Trail of Tears, 40, 43
Trout, William, 11
Tubman, Harriet Ross, 49
Tucker, Mary Lou, 8, 65
Turner, Fredrick, 11
Twain, Mark, (Samuel Clemens), 31
Typhoid, 74

U
Uncle Toms Cabin, (Stowe), 19
Underground Railroad, 49

Unicoi Turnpike, 43
Union Co. GA, 44
United States Flag, 29
University of Wisconsin, 11

V
Vanderbilt, Cornelius, 49

W
Waldo Station, FL, 66, 67
Wartburg, TN. 34
Warwick, Diane, 64
Warwick, Joe, 64
Washington, GA, 48
Washington, George, 36
Wegener, Alfred, 30
White Snakeroot, 20, **21**
    Intoxication, 20
Wilson, Alexander, 17
Wilson, Woodrow Thomas, 39, 51
Wisconsin, 11
Withlacoochee River, 69

Wolfe, Linnie Marsh, 7
Wood, Alphonso, 29, 30
Wood's and Gray's Botany, 29
Worth, Jonathan, 42
Wrightborough Road, 49

Y
Yanu, (Cherokee= bear), 45
Yonah, Mount, 45
York, Alvin Cullum, 29
    Gristmill, 29
    Highway, 29
Yosemite, 6, 11, 30, 51, 70
Yulee, FL, 8, 60, 63, 65, 66
Yulee, David Levy, 63, 67, 71
Yulee Historical Council Inc. 65

Z
Zucker, Monte, 8